THE COMPLETE
PORSCHE

THE COMPLETE
PORSCHE

A MODEL-BY-MODEL HISTORY

BRIAN LABAN

Lowe & B. Hould
Publishers

In memory of
Mary Lear

This edition published in 2004 by Lowe & B. Hould publishers, an imprint of Borders, Inc.,
515 East Liberty, Ann Arbor, MI 48104. Lowe & B. Hould Publishers is a trademark of Borders Properties, Inc.

First published by MBI Publishing Company, Galtier Plaza, Suite 200, 380 Jackson Street, St. Paul, MN 55101-3885 USA

© Salamander Books Ltd. 2003, 2004

An imprint of Chrysalis Books Group

ISBN 0-681-16580-4

Credits
Commissioning Editor: Marie Clayton
Design and Layout: Hardlines Ltd, Charlbury, Oxford
Reproduction: Anorax Imaging Ltd.
Printed in Thailand

The Author
Brian Laban has been a motoring journalist and author since joining the British Automobile Racing Club
as their press officer in the early 1970s. He has worked for several weekly and monthly motoring
magazines and written a number of books covering subjects as diverse as Grand Prix racing and
American cars of the 1950s, or the MGB and the Lamborghini Countach (the latter in the *Supercars*
series, Slamander, 1989). A full-time freelance writer, he now contributes to many of the major motoring
magazines, including *Auto Express*, *Evo*, *GT* and *Purely Porsche*. In 1991 he was the recipient of the Pierre
Dreyfus Award for Outstanding Journalistic Effort.

Contents

Porsche before the Porsche car—the man and his philosophy

At the Paris Motor Show in September 2002, Porsche officially unveiled the production version of one of the most controversial designs in the company's often thought-provoking history. The all-new Cayenne burst into the public gaze as a Porsche with a difference, a big difference—a Porsche to split opinions both among those who might buy it and those who would only ever dream. Cayenne was, in basic terms, Porsche's first ever entry into the "SUV" Sports Utility Vehicle market—or to put it another way, Porsche's first off-roader. But in reality, that's only a detail—the real point of the story isn't so much about the car as about the reaction to it. When Porsche does something new, the world watches, and the world reacts, often quite strongly. Even people who have never actually owned a Porsche apparently feel that they own a stake in the Porsche philosophy, and a say in what Porsche should and shouldn't do.

Over the years, the same phenomenon has shown itself almost every time that Porsche has branched out from its core, sports car product—for which read the 356 in the early days and the 911 family ever after. So anything that hasn't had an air-cooled flat engine behind the rear wheels has started the tongues wagging and polarized opinions. But the funny thing is, once the fuss has died down and people have driven the cars in question, they almost always come to the same conclusion—Porsche still makes great Porsches.

This will not come as a big surprise to those who understand the brand and are aware of its history. Even in the rarefied world of performance cars and supercars, Porsche remains genuinely special, and if ever the over-worked words "classic" and "genius" applied anywhere in the motoring world, they certainly apply to most things Porsche. And that applies both to successive generations of the Porsche family and to the cars they have designed and built—a whole dynasty of brilliant individuals and outstanding cars.

The founder of that dynasty, Ferdinand Porsche, was born in Mattersdorf (in what's now the Czech Republic) in 1875. He was the third son of a tinsmith, and joined the family business after his older brother Anton was killed in a working accident. Before he even saw an automobile he began to tinker with electricity—and with his mother's approval rather than his father's he went to evening classes at the technical school in nearby Reichenberg. Around 1890 he built a complete electrical installation for the family house and workshop, which finally convinced his father that his education wasn't completely wasted—so by 1894 he had moved to Vienna to study part-time (and rather unofficially, as he simply walked into whatever lectures interested him) at the Technical University.

He supported his studies there by working as an apprentice with a local electrical engineering firm, Bela Egger, and by 1898 he was head of their test department. In 1899 he joined Jacob Lohner's automobile company, and in 1900 Ferdinand Porsche's first complete car design was shown at the Paris World's Fair. Characteristically, the Lohner-Porsche was a highly innovative design—an electric car in an age where the competition between petrol, electricity and steam was still not entirely settled. But far more innovative than the simple fact of being powered by electricity was its drive system, comprising four individual hub-mounted motors, giving it both four-wheel drive and something that was to become a Porsche hallmark, remarkable mechanical efficiency.

Within a year the Lohner-Porsche had started another Porsche tradition, as competition versions were built, and successfully campaigned in various trials.

Opposite: From his first days as a designer, Ferdinand Porsche was an innovator. This early creation, the Lohner-Porsche of 1900, features his pioneering electric hub-drive system.

Left: Father, son and new baby. Ferry Porsche, Professor Ferdinand Porsche and the first car to bear the Porsche name—the original 356 Roadster in Gmünd, with Beetle ancestors in background.

Below: Porsche wasted no time in starting to advertise the marque, starting with the earliest cabriolets.

C A B R I O L E T

Die Karosserie bietet zwei Personen bequem Platz und weist hinter den Sitzen einen geräumigen Kofferraum auf, der ebensogut auch für Notsitze von zwei Kindern verwendet werden kann.

Wer auf Reisen den freien, offenen Ausblick auf die Schönheit unserer Bergwelt und Alpenseen, auf die Sehenswürdigkeiten unserer Städte und Dörfer genießen will, dem bietet das

Sport-Cabriolet Typ 356

die Erfüllung seiner Wünsche.

Beiden, im Fahrgestell gleichen Fahrzeugtypen gemeinsam ist eine besondere Sparsamkeit im Betriebsstoffverbrauch. Bei höchster Reisegeschwindigkeit erreicht der Kraftstoffverbrauch nur 7,2 Liter/100 km und kann bei gemäßigter Fahrweise noch erheblich gesenkt werden.

Occasionally, Porsche competed (and did well) with his own designs, and in 1902, as a Reserve Infantryman, he drove Archduke Franz Ferdinand during a demonstration of the Lohner-Porsche for military use.

All of this made certain that the still young Ferdinand Porsche was noticed, and within a few years he had been snapped up as technical director of the Austro-Daimler company, succeeding Paul Daimler and switching without much difficulty from his pioneering electric car designs to more conventional petrol ones. It was the start of a long association, which saw Porsche stay with Austro-Daimler for more than twenty years and rise to the position of chief engineer for the giant Daimler-Benz company that grew out of Austro-Daimler.

Throughout that time, Porsche's reputation was rooted in his designs. He continued to work on petrol-electric "mixed drives," including an 85hp racing car in 1907, which he drove himself. In September 1909 he was driving one of his own racing cars when his son Ferry was born. By 1910 (even before Austria had an airplane maker) he designed aero engines—including, in 1912, an air-cooled flat-four which is widely regarded now as a direct ancestor of his Volkswagen and Porsche car engines. During World War I Porsche designed a road train with Lohner-style hub motors on each carriage—and his C-train, carrying a huge Skoda mortar, was reckoned to be the heaviest motorized gun ever built.

He was already an industry high-flyer and in 1916 he was appointed managing director of Austro-Daimler, honored by the emperor, and received an honorary doctorate from the University of Vienna. With Austria's postwar re-organization he also became a Czech citizen, and stayed that way until 1938, when the Nazi regime obliged him to become a German national.

What he did do between the wars was carry on with his pioneering designs, and especially his sporting designs. In 1922 he designed a very different car from Austro-Daimler's usual line—a much smaller, sporting car for a close friend, Count Sascha Kolowrat, head of Austria's largest film company, who wanted a small sports car for hillclimbs and rallies. Kolowrat financed it, Austro-Daimler grudgingly built it (in very small numbers), and the four-cylinder 1100cc "Sascha" was quick enough to win its class in the 1922 Targa Florio road race.

Early in 1923 Porsche followed Paul Daimler into another post, as a designer for Daimler. Then in 1929 he moved to Austria's biggest car maker, Steyr, as chief engineer and member of the board—albeit for just a few months, until Steyr's bank collapsed and the company was absorbed into Austro-Daimler. That prompted Porsche to leave and start his own design office in Stuttgart—in

Left: As the 1950s turned into the 1960s, the 356 family had already served Porsche for more than a decade, and annual production had reached around 8000 cars, but there was much more to come.

December 1930, as Konstruktionsbüro für Motoren und Fahrzeugbau Dr Ing hc Ferdinand Porsche GmbH. He took his protégé, the brilliant young engineer Karl Rabe, who he had met at Austro-Daimler, with him—and Rabe would be Porsche's chief engineer until 1966. 21-year-old Ferry Porsche, previously apprenticed to Bosch and then Steyr, also joined the original staff of nine, which grew to 13 during 1931 and to around 115, including assembly workers, by 1938.

The bureau had been officially registered in March 1931 but, worrying that the outside world might be concerned by the apparent lack of experience, Porsche labeled its first design (a small car for Wanderer) Project 7.

In September 1931 they started Project 12, a small car for Zundapp, who wanted to use a five-cylinder water-cooled radial engine but soon abandoned the project as too expensive. Porsche, however, adapted some of the work already done for a small car for NSU, with an air-cooled flat-four engine. As NSU motor cycle production boomed—this project was also shelved, but its influence was going to be far reaching. Early in 1934 Porsche was commissioned, by the National Socialist government, to design a low cost "people's car," and Project 60 eventually became the Volkswagen, with air-cooled flat-four power. Having signed the design agreement in June 1934, in 1936 Porsche (working in his own garage) completed the first three prototypes of what would become the world's biggest selling car—and his skills were in greater demand than ever.

In 1932 the Russian government offered him the role of "State Designer," with the promise of almost unlimited resources to develop his own ideas—but Porsche said no. In 1936 he also visited both America and Britain to look at their motor industries, and in 1937, this time with son Ferry, he returned to America and talked about the concept of a "people's car" with Henry Ford. And at the other end of the design spectrum in the late 1930s, but again funded mainly by the Nazi government, Porsche designed the remarkable mid-engined Auto-Union Grand Prix cars—at the time among the most powerful racing cars ever built.

Those designs were officially handled by an independent offshoot of the main design bureau, Hochleistungs Fahrzeugbau GmbH, which Porsche had set up in November 1932—and which had also been planning to build a land speed record challenger. Again in stark contrast, as the approach of World War II killed the record-breaker project, Porsche designed the legendary Tiger tank.

The Volkswagen "Beetle"—arguably the most impressive illustration of Ferdinand Porsche's minimalist design philosophy—was already in limited production by the

outbreak of war, albeit mainly for military users, and although the Porsche design works moved to Gmünd in 1944, Ferdinand remained in Stuttgart. But while the Porsche bureau made other design contributions to the German military machine, Ferdinand Porsche's own relationship with the Nazi regime was very ambivalent. He refused, for instance, to call Adolf Hitler "Fuhrer," and always referred to him as Herr Hitler, staying as far away from the political side of his work as he possibly could. That didn't, however, save him from being arrested by the Americans at the end of the war (in October 1945) and handed over to the French—who allowed Renault to use his services as a consultant, but kept Professor Porsche imprisoned for two years.

His release, in August 1947, was finally funded by the design fees for the postwar Cisitalia Grand Prix car, designed by Ferdinand's son Ferry around an outline suggested by his father, but never actually raced. And coinciding with Porsche senior's release, the company was about to enter its next phase, as a sports car maker in its own right, for the first time under Porsche's own badge.

Project 356 would be a lightweight, open-topped two-seater with a modestly tuned four-cylinder air-cooled Volkswagen engine, Volkswagen-based suspension and an aluminum body, and it would be the foundation for the vast majority of what Porsche has built since. But it was more than just a car; with the 356, Porsche established the philosophy which has seen Porsche design through to the present day—of the balances between weight and power, sophistication and simplicity, style and function. And around that philosophy, Porsche as a company began to grow, and grow fast.

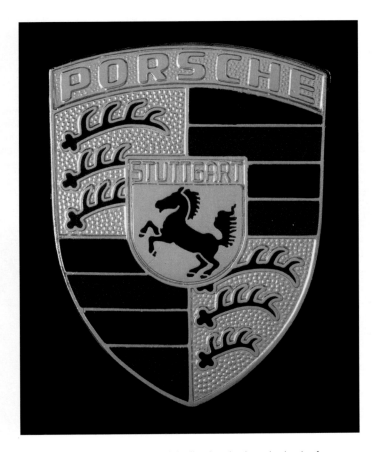

Above: The Porsche badge, originally sketched on the back of a napkin in a New York restaurant by the remarkable Max Hoffman during a business meeting with Ferry Porsche. It combines the crest of the House of Wurtemberg with the prancing horse of the city of Stuttgart—and the Porsche name.

The first fifty 356s were built, virtually by hand, in the tiny factory at Gmünd, but it was soon obvious that production capacity there would be hopelessly inadequate, so Porsche began to negotiate with the military authorities for the return of its Stuttgart works—and between July 1949 and September 1950, they moved back. By then they had around 150 staff and gradually doubled daily production from the planned ten cars a week, to make almost 300 cars during 1950. The 500th Porsche was built in March 1951, and in June Porsche began another long-running chapter with its first entry at Le Mans, as motor sport continued to play its part in proving Porsche designs and promoting Porsche customer cars. It contributed to worldwide recognition and commercial success. By the mid-1950s some 75 per cent of the 3000 or so cars built by Porsche's now 600-strong workforce were being sold in the USA.

The 10,000th Porsche would be built in March 1956 and by the end of the 1950s annual production was almost 8000 cars. That was already hugely more than Ferdinand Porsche had ever expected to achieve with his own marque, but he had not lived to see it. He died, after suffering a stroke, in January 1951—but his company's future was already in good hands, as son Ferry had in effect been running its affairs since his father's wartime internment. And now, Ferry would continue his father's philosophy through Porsche's cars…

Above: Ferry Porsche in later life. Ferry had worked almost all his life with his father Ferdinand, followed very similar design principles, and was a natural successor as head of the company when his father died in 1951.

Below: What it's all about. The classic Porsche layout, an air-cooled horizontally-opposed engine set out behind the gearbox and rear axle, in this case in the classic first generation Turbo. The details changed but the minimalist design philosophy has never wavered.

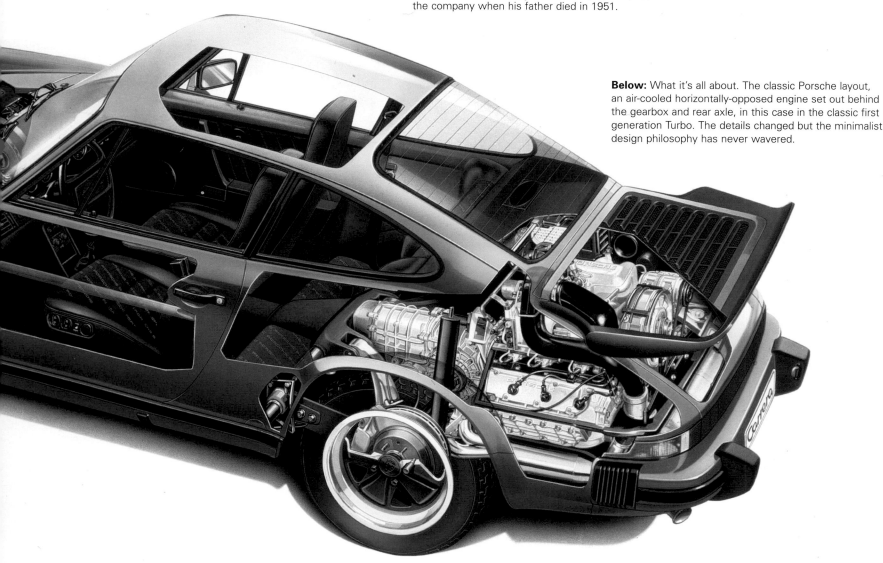

SPECIFICATIONS

Engine Flat-four, air-cooled
Capacity 1131cc
Bore x stroke 75.0 x 64.0mm
Compression ratio 6.5:1
Power 35–40bhp
Valve gear Single central camshaft, pushrods
Fuel system Single Solex 26VFJ downdraft carburetor
Transmission Four-speed manual
Front suspension Independent, by trailing arms, transverse torsion bars, telescopic dampers
Rear suspension Independent, by swing axle, transverse torsion bars, lever-action dampers (reversed VW Beetle suspension)
Brakes All drums, mechanically operated
Wheels Bolt-on, steel disc
Weight 1289lb. (585kg)
Maximum speed 84mph (135kph)
Production One (prototype), June 1948

356 Roadster

Project number 356 was a major Porsche milestone. It hit the drawing boards in mid-July 1947, and after all the designs that had gone before, and the broad brush of products for a catalogue of outside clients, this one was different. It was for Porsche themselves, and it was to be a car—the first to bear Porsche's own name. It was a sign that the Porsche operation was moving forwards, but in the run-up to Project 356, things had been fairly fraught.

The design office had moved near the end of the war from Stuttgart to a temporary (and very cramped) home in Gmünd in southern Austria, run initially by Ferdinand Porsche's daughter, Louise. Her brother, Ferry, had been released from brief internment by the French in July 1946, but although the charges against him were tenuous, their father, Professor Ferdinand, wasn't freed until the following year. In the meantime, Ferry had helped fund both the

Right: The simple rear hatch did not even have a cooling grille. The VW-derived engine was set ahead of the four-speed gearbox, which also changed the VW rear suspension from trailing to leading link, and led to problems with the torsion bar mountings.

company and his father's "bail" by designing the Cisitalia GP car for Italian industrialist Piero Dusio, and although the mid-engined four-wheel-drive car never raced it showed that Porsche design had lost none of its talent for innovation.

When Ferdinand was released, in August 1947, he soon added his ideas for the 356 to those of Ferry, who had done the initial drawings with chief designer Karl Rabe. Not surprisingly, the design drew heavily on Porsche's best-known earlier work, the VW Beetle. That meant minimum weight, optimum aerodynamic form, and maximum simplicity. The first Porsche would be, in effect, a sports car built around the bones of the Beetle—notably its engine, transmission, brakes, suspension and steering, plus many smaller components. Most would be subtly upgraded, but the objectives Porsche had pursued with the Beetle—solid performance and durability for a tightly controlled price—would be just as appropriate for the more sporty Project 356. Because 356 was a sports car.

As big a problem as designing it was building it, because although the VW had gone into production immediately after the war, Beetle components, even basic materials, were far from easy to come by—even for the

Top: The unique mid-engined layout of the 356-1 made the cockpit a strict two-seater, with no space behind the seats.

Below: The backward slope of the headlight units mirrored that on the Beetle, and became a Porsche hallmark.

man who had designed the car. But eventually Porsche put together enough leftover prototype parts and hard-won new ones to turn the 356 drawings into reality.

It further refined the Beetle philosophy of using light weight and a slippery shape to make the most of modest power—although not quite as modest as the original VW. The air-cooled 1131cc flat-four engine gained slightly bigger valves and a higher compression ratio to lift power from 25 to 35bhp, and with a second downdraft carburetor to 40bhp. The clutch and non-syncro four-speed gearbox were virtually unchanged, but for the two-seater 356 Roadster the engine/transmission assembly was turned back to front compared with the Beetle to give a mid- rather than rear-engined layout—just what Porsche had long favored for motor racing designs.

It had its drawbacks, mainly in reversing the rear suspension to become leading rather than trailing link, with its transverse torsion bars awkwardly sited at the back of the chassis. The front suspension, cable-operated drum brakes and worm and roller steering were almost unchanged Beetle carry-overs—but in a competition-style tubular steel chassis that was very different from the VW's pressed-steel platform and on a considerably shorter wheelbase.

The open two-seater body was as simple as the mechanical elements, and for the same reasons—shortage of materials and an aversion to unnecessary weight. Aside from lacking a roof it closely resembled an aluminum-bodied competition coupe version of the VW that Porsche had designed in 1939, for the Berlin to Rome road race that never actually took place, thanks to the war.

The 356 body was aluminum, too, designed by Erwin Komenda and hand-formed by coachbuilder Friedrich Weber. Its aerodynamic cleanness is still obvious more than fifty years on, and so is the start of a trademark Porsche "look," especially around the nose and in the understated detail.

Above: The roadster's dashboard gave just enough information for a competition role, but a tachometer was not normally fitted to the first coupes—and the badge was not designed until later.

Above: The interior trim on the early cars was minimal, but was designed for practicality.

Above: Handmade body fittings, such as the rear light, show Porsche's talent for combining function with style.

Below: Body designer Komenda's quest for minimal aerodynamic drag shows in clever detailing—such as the flush door handles.

SPECIFICATIONS

Engine Flat-four, air-cooled
Capacity 1086cc
Bore x stroke 73.5 x 64.0mm
Compression ratio 7.0:1
Power 40bhp
Valve gear Single central camshaft, pushrods
Fuel system Two downdraft Solex 32PBIC carburetors
Transmission Four-speed manual
Front suspension Independent, by trailing arms, transverse torsion bars, telescopic dampers
Rear suspension Independent, by swing axle, transverse torsion bars, telescopic dampers
Brakes All drums; originally mechanically operation, all later cars have hydraulic operation
Wheels Bolt-on, steel disc
Weight 1642lb. (745kg)
Maximum speed 87mph (140kph)
Production 4670, 1100 coupes, 1950-54

356 Coupe

The first Porsche was finished on 8 June 1948 and numbered 356-1. Weighing only 585kg and with its slippery shape, it was impressively quick even with only 40bhp (including a top speed of almost 85mph), and its light weight also contributed to good braking and neat handling. In fact within weeks, 356-1, driven by Ferry's cousin Herbert Kaes, had scored the Porsche marque's first competition success, with a class win in a race in Innsbruck. And although it was a never-to-be-repeated one-off model, its successors were already under development, as Porsche edged towards true series production.

From 356-1 to a genuine production 356 was a more complicated step than it might at first sound, but it happened pretty quickly given the circumstances. 356-1 had been a successful design insofar as performance and driveability were concerned, but it did have its shortcomings, notably with the "back-to-front" rear suspension layout. And with their limited production facilities in Gmünd, plus the ongoing shortage of parts and materials, Porsche would never be able to build the design in any meaningful numbers—so they changed it.

They kept the fundamentals (the VW-based engine, transmission, brakes, steering and suspension) but changed the packaging, concentrating on making the car buildable in reasonable numbers. They found much-needed financial and logistical backing from two Swiss businessmen called Senger and Blank, who ran a Zurich-based advertising agency and helped Porsche acquire a limited supply of VW parts from the Swiss VW agency (which had been set up in 1945). Porsche also found supplies of sheet aluminum from Switzerland, for bodies, but Austria would only let them import it if they could export the cars it went into. Those included 356-1, and the first four "production" cars, all aluminum-bodied coupes which (thanks to Herr Senger) went back to Switzerland.

They were still called 356 but were very different from 356-1, and not only in body style. The difficult and expensive to build tubular frame had been replaced by a pressed-steel platform similar to the Beetle's but shorter in the wheelbase and considerably stiffer, although still light enough to be lifted by one man. Equally fundamentally, the engine was turned round again to sit as it did in the VW, behind the gearbox. That put the engine right at the back of the car and sacrificed some of the mid-engine's ideal balance (compensated for by putting things like battery, fuel tank and spare wheel in the front), but made the rear suspension packaging much more reliable. It also created space for a reasonable amount of luggage (or hardy passengers) behind the front seats, and moved the noisiest bits further away from the cabin. All of which made the production 356 altogether more user-friendly than the 356-1 prototype.

What survived was the essential character—light weight and fine aerodynamics for decent performance, and optimum simplicity, now for production purposes as well as for reliability and dynamics. Komenda did the bodywork again, and the classic fastback coupe shape speaks for itself. The earliest cars had split windscreens and separate front quarterlights, and there were many

Top Left: The body swept down into a fastback tail and engine cover. Details such as lights and bumpers would change from time to time, but the classic 356 coupe shape was already all but set.

Middle Left: The racing style mirror on this car was probably not an original fitting.

Middle Right: The cockpit and dashboard of the early 356 coupes, such as this 1951 model, was more hospitable than the Spartan interior of the 356-1.

Below: Erwin Komenda was again responsible for the body styling, and his first coupe was very similar to the roadster up to the waistline.

other detail differences between early aluminum-bodied 356s and the later steel-bodied ones, especially around the tail. There were even small variations from car to car in the early, "hand-built" days, but that was more about improving quality by experience than about compromising quality by method—in all major respects the 356 shape was already established.

Mechanical detail varied too, not least because of the early supply limitations. A few cars used the original 1131cc capacity but a shorter-stroke 1086cc was soon standardized (suiting the 1100 racing classes). Power was still 40bhp, but although the coupe was slightly heavier than the one-off Roadster (leading to stronger Lockheed brakes) it had even lower drag, so it was still good for around 85mph—if not with quite such crisp acceleration.

And as the car evolved, so did the company. Crucially, from September 1948 Porsche became official design consultants and Austrian agents to VW, received a 5DM royalty on every Beetle sold—and perhaps most important of all, guaranteed themselves a more regular supply of essential VW components.

That set production growing (although Gmünd output to early 1951 would only total 46 cars) and prompted moves to take the larger Stuttgart premises back from the Americans who had leased them since the war. Until that happened, in 1955, Porsche arranged for Stuttgart-based Reutter Carrosserie to supply bodyshells and lease Porsche some space in the Reutter works for mechanical assembly. Biggest change of all, bodies would now be in steel, not aluminum, but when the first German-built Porsche was completed early in 1950, at least it looked almost exactly like its Gmünd-built cousins.

Under the skin it was already changing again. April 1951 and the Frankfurt Show saw a 44bhp 1300cc option, the Paris Show six months later added a 1500 option. And by then Porsche had already built more than double the 500 cars that they had originally expected to build.

Below: The first body style, with the two-piece windscreen, survived until 1952. When production moved from Gmünd to Stuttgart, the two 'screen panels were made slightly curved rather than flat.

Far Left: Even at this very early stage, the logo style was already fixed.

Left: The flat-four, air-cooled engine, while unashamedly Beetle-derived, soon started to become more Porsche and less VW, a shorter stroke giving 1086cc for most cars—to qualify for 1100cc racing classes. A 1300cc engine, with 10 per cent more power, was offered in 1951.

SPECIFICATIONS

Engine Flat-four, air-cooled
Capacity 1488cc (smaller
  capacity cars also built)
Bore x stroke 80.0 x 74.0mm
Compression ratio 8.2:1
Power 70bhp
Valve gear Single central
  camshaft, pushrods
Fuel system Two downdraft
  Solex 32PBIC carburetors
Transmission Four-speed
  manual
Front suspension Independent,
  by trailing arms, transverse
  torsion bars, telescopic
  dampers
Rear suspension Independent,
  by swing axle, transverse
  torsion bars, lever-type
  dampers
Brakes All drums
Wheels Bolt-on, steel disc
Weight 1410lb. (640kg)
Maximum speed 101mph
  (162kph)
Production 5 cars converted
  from Gmünd coupes, 1951

356 Lightweight Coupe

Having seen the potential of 356-1, Porsche were taking motor sport seriously—not least for the technical and commercial advantages it offered. And weighing up the relative benefits of conventional advertising or exposure through motor sport, Porsche decided that motor sport would be their front-line advertising.

Private owners had already started racing and rallying their 356s, and winning. Now, while the steel-bodied 356s from Stuttgart carried production to new levels, the early aluminum-bodied ones from Gmünd were exactly what Porsche needed to take the international motor sport stage. They were light, and their slightly narrower cabins

with less drag were another bonus, because Porsche had chosen to make their big-time debut at a race where both light weight and a slippery shape were vital, especially in the smaller engined classes. Porsche were about to make their first visit to Le Mans.

Two influences were drawing them towards the famous endurance race: Auguste Veuillet and Charles Faroux. Veuillet was the French Porsche importer, and reasoned that Le Mans and Porsche were made for each other. Veteran French motoring journalist Faroux was an old friend of Professor Porsche's, and had helped arrange his release from French internment after the war.

Right: Even without the racing numbers on the doors, the shape of the lightweight coupe left little doubt as to its mission in life. The covered wheel arches were clearly aimed at optimum dynamics.

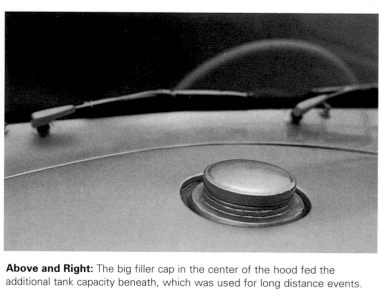

Above and Right: The big filler cap in the center of the hood fed the additional tank capacity beneath, which was used for long distance events.

As editor of La Vie Automobile in the 1920s, Faroux had also conceived the Le Mans 24-Hour race itself. In October 1950 he visited Porsche in Stuttgart, to suggest that the marque enter Le Mans in 1951. In March, Veuillet proved that his own 356 coupe could lap the Montlhéry track outside Paris at over 90mph, Porsche were officially invited to race in the 24 Hours, and accepted.

They planned to send three 1086cc Gmünd coupes for the 1100cc class—modified to give 46bhp, but also tuned with an eye to reliability. At 640kg the aluminum-bodied coupes shaved some 110kg off the steel-bodied 356, while the aerodynamic advantage of the narrower roof was supplemented by faired wheel arches and smooth panels under both nose and tail. With about 72bhp per tonne they would top 100mph—and they had all the 356's other virtues of agile handling and strong braking. For endurance, fuel capacity was increased to 78 liters by extending the tank around the front-mounted spare wheel, with a quick-fill cap fitted in the middle of the strapped-down front bonnet. There were additional driving lights on the nose, but the drum brakes and torsion bar suspension were only mildly uprated and Porsche were ready to go.

Or not quite, because having recruited German former Le Mans driver Paul von Guilleaume to manage the team, Porsche lost three cars to accidents even before qualifying for Le Mans began. So the planned three-car team was reduced to one car, incorporating salvaged parts from several of the others but nominally the tenth of the first series 356s from Gmünd.

It was entrusted to Veuillet and fellow Frenchman Edmond Mouchet, both with previous Le Mans experience. It was a fine debut. They averaged 73.6mph with a fastest lap of 87mph, finished twentieth overall and, most impressively, won the 1100cc class—ahead of the winner of the 1500 class. They won the class again in 1952, and except for 1959 and 1965 Porsche scored Le Mans class wins in every year until they started their record run of outright wins in 1970.

The lightweight coupes also amassed further glories. In August 1951 von Guilleaume and Count Heinz von der Muhle (using a secret 1488cc engine) took their class (and a remarkable third overall) in the grueling Liège-Sofia-Liège Rally; in October one car with the normal 1086cc engine and one with the new 1488cc (giving up to 72bhp) set short- and long-distance records at Montlhéry. The 1100 ran for 500 miles in six hours, at up to 101.4mph; the 1500 set a world record average of 95.2mph over 72 hours and more than 6850 miles—after which it went to the Paris Salon to help introduce a 60bhp 1500 engine option for the production 356 coupe. Motor sport as advertising, exactly as planned.

And with continuous development, the lightweight coupes raced and rallied well into the mid-1950s, recording dozens of outright and class wins—including the 1952 Coppa Inter-Europa at Monza, the Sestrière Rally, GP of Belgrade and Rallye des Alpes in 1953, and greatest of all, in the Liège-Rome-Liège Rally (effectively a 3200-mile road race taking in 33 Alpine passes) in both 1952 and 1954. Soon, the experimental four-cam 1500 engine used in the 1954 Liège winner was to be seen in everything from the Carrera to a new F2 car. For Porsche, racing was proving to be a very good way to go.

Far Left: The nose of this coupe, with the small grille and strapped down hood, is almost identical to the form in which the model first appeared at Le Mans in 1951.

Left: Light weight, not luxury, was the aim of the aluminum body, and details such as the simple, strap-operated side windows, saved precious pounds in weight.

Below: The louvered rear side windows helped to cool down both the engine and the cockpit.

Below: Although it still had the VW flat-four as its starting point, the first Porsche "production" racer also had new camshafts, further improved cylinder heads and improved carburation.

SPECIFICATIONS

356A 1600S Coupe

Engine Flat-four, air-cooled

Capacity 1582cc

Bore x stroke 82.5 x 74.0mm

Compression ratio 8.5:1

Power 75bhp

Valve gear Single central camshaft, pushrods

Fuel system Two downdraft Solex 40PBIC carburetors

Transmission Four-speed manual

Front suspension Independent, by trailing arms, transverse torsion bars, telescopic dampers, anti-roll bar

Rear suspension Independent, by swing axle, transverse torsion bars, telescopic dampers

Brakes All drums

Wheels Bolt-on, steel disc (center-lock optional)

Weight 1940lb. (880kg)

Maximum speed 112mph (180kph)

Production 5981 (incuding all body styles), 1956–9

Above: The 356's lines had developed subtly; the 356A had a curved one-piece windshield.

Below: Wheel size had been reduced from 16-inch to 15-inch, which gave a squatter, more modern look.

In March 1956, only eight years after hand building 356-1 in Gmünd, Porsche's 10,000th production car was driven off the Stuttgart line by Ferry's youngest son, Wolfgang—during a party celebrating the 25th anniversary of Dr Ing hc F Porsche GmbH. The car was a 356A coupe and as original 356 production plans had anticipated no more than 500 cars, there was plenty to celebrate. That figure of 500 represented the first order of steel shells from Reutter, placed in November 1949. The shells would cost 200,000DM—precisely the same figure as Porsche's initial working capital. And another happy coincidence: early in 1950 Porsche had shown a 356 coupe and Beutler cabrio to VW dealers in Wolfsburg, taken orders for 37 cars, and deposits amounting to almost exactly 200,000DM. So serious 356 production started in 1950, as postwar economies continued to recover and buying a sports car (especially a German one) became less of an eccentricity. But all those early cars were destined for Europe, and another market was about to change Porsche's outlook very dramatically.

At the Paris Show in October 1950, Professor Porsche met Max Hoffman, an American citizen of Austrian descent, a New York car dealer with a love of sports cars, and the man who would take Porsche into the American market. Which was the real key to an extraordinary growth in production numbers.

Porsche passed its original notion of 500 356s in March 1951; in August they built the 1000th; March 1954 brought number 5000; number 10,000 was the car at the center of that March 1956 celebration. And the key to all of this had been Porsche's success in America, promoted by Max Hoffman.

Hoffman was a flamboyant salesman, brilliant businessman, and outstanding judge of what sells. In the early 1950s, helped by rave reviews, conspicuous competition success, and Max, Porsches were about to become the car for the American sporty driver. Soon, half Porsche's production was going to America, and by the late 1950s exports would be closer to 70 per cent. And while that gave Porsche fantastic sales, it also gave America a considerable say in what Porsche should build. Or rather it gave Max a big say. But in that he understood Porsche to the extent that he did, that was hardly a problem.

It was, though, instrumental in how the 356 evolved. While keeping its core character it gained power, performance, more flexibility for more relaxed manners, better brakes to match the performance, and improved suspension to benefit both roadholding and ride comfort. Porsches were already far more Porsche than VW. By 1951 the flat-four engine had new alloy heads with inclined exhaust valves, and a change from steel-lined cylinders to alloy barrels with hard chrome-plated bores offered significant weight savings, plus the chance to increase capacity from 1086cc to 1286cc—the options on offer by late 1952. They were joined by a new 1500 alternative, created by lengthening the stroke for the first and last time in the original VW-style block. Or more accurately, two 1488cc options—the original (designed for competition) with a complex and expensive "built-up" crankshaft with roller bearings, the other with conventional one-piece forged crank in plain bearings. And although both were catalogue options, the roller-type (with a bit more power but less refinement and flexibility and an appetite for more frequent maintenance—not to mention the original cost) was kept for the Super, while the cheaper, smoother, plain-bearing version was much the more common choice in the standard 356.

Because there was no way of stretching the stroke any further, 1488cc was as far as capacity could go with the original, pushrod block, before it was changed to allow still bigger bores and a capacity of 1582cc in 1955. That gave 70bhp with plain crankshaft or 88bhp with rollers, backed by improvements for handling, comfort and safety. Those had also been an ongoing process: twin leading-shoe brakes

with bigger finned drums from 1951; one-piece windscreens and superb new all-syncromesh gearboxes from 1952; more instrumentation, reclining front and folding rear seats from around 1953; and so it went on.

By 1956 the windscreen had more wraparound, wheels were smaller diameter but wider, torsion bars were slightly softer with more suspension travel, controlled by better dampers and a front anti-roll bar. The 356, in short, was acknowledging American tastes without losing its European roots. And in 1956 the extent of the cumulative development was acknowledged when the car was renamed as the 356A, in Coupe, Cabriolet and Speedster styles. And the Speedster takes us neatly back to Max Hoffman…

Below: The twin round tail-lights only survived on the 356A through the 1956 model year and the early part of 1957.

Above: The rear side windows were now glass.

Above Right: Refinements to the details were made for the American market.

Right: The interior now had a padded dashboard and fully-reclining front seats.

Below Right: Folding rear seat backs created more versatile accommodation.

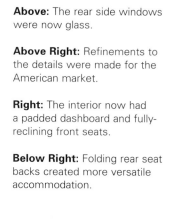

356A 1600 Speedster

SPECIFICATIONS

Engine Flat-four, air-cooled
Capacity 1582cc
Bore x stroke 82.5 x 74.0mm
Compression ratio 7.5:1
Power 60bhp
Valve gear Single central camshaft, pushrods
Fuel system Two downdraft Solex 32PBIC carburetors
Transmission Four-speed manual
Front suspension Independent, by trailing arms, transverse torsion bars, telescopic dampers, anti-roll bar
Rear suspension Independent, by swing axle, transverse torsion bars, telescopic dampers
Brakes All drums
Wheels Bolt-on, steel disc (center-lock optional)
Weight 1840lb. (835kg)
Maximum speed 100mph (160kph)
Production n/a (incuded in 356A total), 1956–9

In the 1950s, Max Hoffman became a legend among auto enthusiasts in America. After the war, his Park Avenue, New York dealership almost single-handedly re-opened America to European cars, and especially to European sports cars—from VW to Mercedes, and from BMW to Porsche. And with his Austrian ancestry, Max was definitely a friend of the Porsche marque.

At the Paris Show in October 1950 he met Professor Porsche, now 75 and in failing health, and arranged to import the first Porsches into America. A few months later, on 30 January 1951, having suffered a stroke and being bed-ridden since November, Ferdinand Porsche died. But thanks to Ferry, who was already running the Porsche companies, the relationship with Hoffman survived—and ultimately, Porsche's huge sales success in America was built on it.

But Max was far more than just a car salesman. In 1952 he brokered a deal for Porsche to act as consultants to Studebaker, and to design a sporty car for them, with aerodynamic styling and a rear-mounted air-cooled six-cylinder engine. Partly because of Studebaker's lack of technical resources, partly because of an attack of conservatism, largely because they were in dire financial trouble and about to be absorbed by Packard, the car didn't happen—but the project did strengthen the

relationship between Hoffman and Porsche. Hosting Ferry during his second post-war visit to America Max suggested that Porsche needed a proper badge, and in a New York restaurant Ferry sketched one on the back of a napkin—the crest of the house of Wurtemberg, the prancing black horse of the city of Stuttgart, and the Porsche name. Komenda tidied the sketch up and within a year it had become the official Porsche badge—and still is.

But what Max loved most was sports cars, and sports cars he knew the American market would buy, in big numbers. It was Max who suggested to Mercedes in 1953 that they turned their 300SL racer into a roadgoing supercar, and his 1000 firm orders overcame their reluctance to produce it. So the legendary Gullwing made its debut at the 1954 New York Show, and soon after Max suggested a new version of the 356, aimed right at young America.

The idea was to bring down both weight and price, deleting anything the car didn't totally need, giving it a distinctive look, and selling it as a sporty special edition at an aggressive price. The Speedster was born.

Porsche didn't mind that it was originally intended for America-only, the numbers would add up anyway and the work required wasn't huge. Reutter built it, leaving the 356 cabriolet essentially unchanged below the waist, lowering the windscreen by 88mm, raking it right back in a

Below: The Speedster's distinctive "inverted bathtub" lines probably weren't the sort of thing that Porsche would ever have drawn themselves, but they trusted Max Hoffman's knowledge of the U.S. market implicitly, and Max was soon given his chopped-down 356 hot-rod.

slim chrome frame rather than the usual body-colored pressing, and matching it with a chopped down (and more or less token) soft-top. There were neat chrome strips on the flanks, plastic sidescreens instead of wind-up windows, bucket seats, a minimalist dashboard, and not much else. But in the Speedster, as Max knew, less was more.

It was lighter than the cabrio, geared for sparkling acceleration, with its lower center of gravity it handled well, and it sold for just $2995 ex-New York. But what really made it work wasn't low price, it was high style.

Not that it wasn't a real sports car, or a real Porsche. The first 1500 or 1500S versions had 55 or 70bhp and would top 100mph. The later Carrera Speedster had the option of 100 or 110bhp from the race-bred four-cam engine, and in 1957 the GT Carrera Speedster had brakes, steering, suspension and engine closely related to the racing Spyder, less weight again with many aluminum panels, lighter seats and even less trim, and it was even faster.

It was the swansong. The Speedster had been offered in Europe as well as America, and sold well; it echoed the 356A with 1600 and 1600S engines, but never reached 1600 Carrera form. In 1958 it was reincarnated for Europe as the 356 Convertible D, bodied by Drauz of Heilbronn, but diluting the Spartan feel and caricature styling of the original, and its affordability. As the 356B-based Roadster D from 1960 to 1963 the purity slipped even further. What it had finally lost was actually irreplaceable—the Max Hoffman touch.

Left: The "windswept" graphics and chrome strip running the length of the body, along the line of the door handle, contrived to give the car a longer and lower look for minimal outlay.

Above: Even with the minimalist approach, the Speedster's painted-metal dash looked good, and it offered all the information a sporty driver would ever need to know—including a rev-counter in the center, a 120mph speedometer and the familiar combined fuel-level and oil-temperature gauge.

Below: Although trim and equipment had been reduced to basics to save weight and cost, items such as the swoopy mirrors added flamboyant style.

Above: In open-topped form—either Speedster or cabriolet—the 356 needed some reshaping around the tail to provide the clearance for the engine cooling fan that the coupe's fastback line accommodated more naturally. Bucket seats and minimal trim distinguish the cockpit.

SPECIFICATIONS

Engine Flat-four, air-cooled
Capacity 1582cc
Bore x stroke 82.5 x 74.0mm
Compression ratio 9.0:1
Power 90bhp
Valve gear Single central
 camshaft, pushrods
Fuel system Two twin-choke
 downdraft Solex 40PII-4
 carburetors
Transmission Four-speed
 manual
Front suspension Independent,
 by trailing arms, transverse
 torsion bars, telescopic
 dampers, anti-roll bar
Rear suspension Independent,
 by swing axle, transverse
 torsion bars, telescopic
 dampers
Brakes All drums
Wheels Bolt-on, steel disc
Weight 1995lb. (905kg)
Maximum speed 110mph
 (176kph)
Production 5694 (all body
 styles), 1960–63

356B Super 90 Roadster

It's a Porsche truth that looks might not change much, but under the skin the changes never stop—and that applied from the beginning. The 356's evolution was already underway when it switched from hand-made aluminum to series-built steel bodies, and continued with the Porsche-built inclined-valve alloy cylinder heads as early as 1949. 1950 brought hydraulic brakes, 1951 the linerless chrome-plated aluminum cylinder barrels to liberate more capacity, and the same year saw a longer stroke and built-up roller bearing crankshaft creating the first 1500 engine—with power growing all the time.

Similar effort went into the chassis as the 356 grew more powerful and quicker. In quick succession, Porsche introduced twin-leading-shoe brakes at the front, and telescopic dampers at the rear replacing the old lever-arm type. So now the 356 went quicker, cornered and rode better, and stopped harder.

If you looked carefully, it changed visibly without changing dramatically. In 1952 the split windscreen was replaced by a one-piece type, still with distinctive center-vee shape; the bumpers moved slightly clear of the body; a rev-counter, clock and fuel gauge were added to a dash which

Below: The 356B Roadster, with its chrome-framed windshield, had something of the character of the earlier generation Speedster in its lines, but with a good deal more refinement—and at a considerably higher price.

originally only sported a speedometer and a radio joined the options list. Reclining front seats and foldable rear-seat backs added space for small passengers or a reasonable amount of luggage; the 55bhp plain-bearing 1500 engine and Porsche-syncromesh gearbox were introduced, while the 70bhp roller crank engine powered the 1500S, for Super—as the milder and more refined plain-bearing 1500 gained the nickname Damen, or ladies; and Ferry's New York-napkin badge design now graced the nose.

By comparison, 1953 was a quieter year—literally, as one of the few changes brought improved sound

insulation for the cabin. As with the 1500, the 1300 was offered in plain and roller crank "S" versions, while the following year brought the American-inspired Speedster. Things disappeared, too—notably the faithful 1100 engine, further distancing Porsche from anything but notional VW connections as Porsche engines adopted a very different three-piece aluminum crankcase design rather than the original two-piece magnesium alloy VW type.

By the 1956 model year the 356 had changed sufficiently to be re-labeled 356A (Porsche don't rush into overstating change). But what was new was creating a

Below: The Roadster was considerably better trimmed and equipped inside than the Speedster had ever been.

Above: The small grilles by the protruding side lights cover the horns.

more modern, more user-friendly car: there were smaller changes, like new door handles, windscreen washers as standard and repositioned heater controls (moved from dash to floor tunnel). There were cosmetic tweaks, a flatter, wider windscreen; and serious mechanical changes, like more compliant but still brilliantly controlled suspension, now with front anti-roll bar, improving both ride and handling; there were further improved gearboxes, and wider, new generation tires on smaller diameter wheels. More power again, too, with the first of the 1600s—although their main benefit was really in flexibility.

1957 saw minor cosmetic changes including neat one-piece tail-lamps, before 1958 brought another rush. A new plain-bearing 1600 engine ousted the roller-bearing type as the original plain-bearing retreated to mainly cast-iron construction, making it heavier but quieter—and cheaper. The wider tires had made the steering heavier, a new steering box and bigger steering wheel made it lighter again, alongside clutch and gearshift changes which made those lighter to operate, too—all to create not just a

Below: Teardrop rear lights and substantial over-riders on the raised bumpers help identify the 356B.

sports car but a civilized sports car. And the looks changed subtly again, as the tailpipes were re-routed through the bottoms of the rear bumper overriders, tidying up the looks and giving better ground clearance but blackening the tail rather quickly.

Then, at the 1959 Frankfurt Show, Porsche introduced its 1960 cars, and the nomenclature reached 356B. This time the cosmetic changes were dramatic—with higher bumpers above front-brake cooling slots, and deeper glass all round, for a lighter interior. Rear space was improved with split-fold rear-seat backs, luggage space in the nose was increased, transmissions and suspension were improved—the latter to reduce roll without having

to stiffen the ride. And for the first time on a 356, radial tires were offered as standard.

A new engine option, the 1600 Super 90, named for its 90bhp output, bridged the gap to the four-cam Carrera but with much better road manners and a less scary pricetag. You could also combine that with a Roadster body—the latest European descendant of the Speedster, but with far more creature comforts and at the top of the price range not the bottom. It saw the 356 range through to the 356C for 1964, by which time Porsche had built well over 76,000 356s, including almost 31,000 356Bs. But now they were already working on something that was originally called the 901…

Left: The fully-trimmed hood was a far cry from the Speedster's.

SPECIFICATIONS

Engine Flat-four, air-cooled
Capacity 1588cc
Bore x stroke 87.5 x 66.0mm
Compression ratio 9.8:1
Power 135bhp
Valve gear Two overhead
camshafts per cylinder bank
Fuel system Two twin-choke
downdraft Weber carburetors
Transmission Four-speed
manual
Front suspension Independent,
by trailing arms, transverse
torsion bars, telescopic
dampers, anti-roll bar
Rear suspension Independent,
by swing axle, transverse
torsion bars, telescopic
dampers
Brakes All drums (some later
converted to discs)
Wheels Bolt-on, steel disc
Weight 1715lb. (778kg)
Maximum speed 137mph
(220kph)
Production 20, 1960–62

356B Carrera GTL Abarth

Above: The engine of the 356B Carrera GTL Abarth ranged from the four-cam flat-four 1600 in standard 115bhp trim, to the 2-liter Carrera 2 engine, with up to 185bhp.

Below: The Abarth was more beetle-backed than the standard Carrera.

Late in 1946, two old friends visited Ferry Porsche, recently released from internment, at the Porsche family home in Zell am Zee. Before the war engineer Rudolf Hruska had been closely involved with the VW project while former motor cycle racer Carlo Abarth had returned from his adopted Austria to his birthplace in Yugoslavia—helped by Ferry's brother-in-law Dr Anton Piëch, whose secretary had become Abarth's wife. Hruska and Abarth had met in Merano in northern Italy, where Abarth had moved after the war, and where his family originated. Hruska had been in nearby Brescia early in 1945, unable to return to Stuttgart as the Americans moved in. The visit to Zell am See was to negotiate the rights to represent Porsche in Italy—once Porsche had something to sell.

The pair had a commercial partner in Italy, Piero Dusio, a former athlete and football star who, before the war, had made a substantial fortune, first in the textile industry then in banking, hotels and sports equipment—the latter as Consorzio Industriale Sportivo Italia, or Cisitalia. Dusio was also a racing driver and sponsor. During the war, with Fiat engineer Dante Giacosa, he planned a family of Fiat-powered "off-the-shelf" single-seater and sports racing cars. After the war they became successful both competitively and commercially, while Cisitalia also built sporty road cars—and planned a GP car.

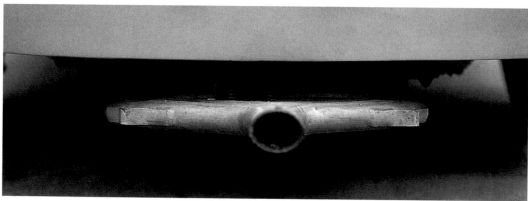

Top Above: The scorpion on the Abarth's badge was from Carlo Abarth's birth sign.

Above: The single, central exhaust system was one of Carlo Abarth's commercial specialities.

Below: Variations in the shape of the side windows were largely a result of the aluminum shells being hand-built. There were literally dozens of cooling vents cut into the engine cover.

Enter legendary racer Tazio Nuvolari, one of the few drivers ever to master Professor Porsche's prewar Auto-Union GP cars, looking for the car with which to resume his career. Nuvolari was introduced to Hruska, both agreed that Porsche could design the car, Hruska and Abarth realized that Dusio could fund it, and through mutual friends made contact. It was subsequently agreed that Porsche (under Ferry's stewardship) would design the GP car, a sports car, even a tractor, for and funded by Dusio. The payments would also cover the bond to expedite Ferdinand Porsche's release from internment.

Ferry's GP car was technically brilliant (with supercharged mid-mounted engine and four-wheel drive) but the project was overtaken by spiraling costs and bankruptcy for Cisitalia. Dusio's attempt to resurrect the company and car in Argentina in 1949 also failed but, post-Cisitalia, former chief mechanic Abarth founded his own company in Turin in April 1949, to build competition cars and tuning equipment under the badge of his birth sign, the scorpion.

Abarth quickly built strong links with Fiat, a prosperous "bolt-on" equipment market, and a fine reputation as a racing car manufacturer. And he maintained his personal contacts with the Porsche family, until 1960 brought them back into technical partnership—in a car with which Porsche could contest the GT category of the World Championship for Makes.

The lightweight coupe was the 356B Carrera GTL Abarth, based on the production 356B Carrera, whose mechanical specification, including the standard wheelbase, survived largely unchanged under the slippery new bumperless, long-nosed, low-roofed aluminum shell. There are arguments over who designed and built those (and some amusement over the standard of Turin workmanship versus Stuttgart's), but the aerodynamic shape worked, and the GTL Abarth saved more than 135kg over a steel-bodied Carrera.

Porsche supplied 21 chassis in 1960, of which apparently only 18 were originally built up—and no two were precisely identical. The trailing-arm torsion-bar

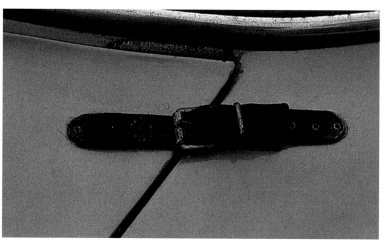

Left: With its strapped-down hood, there wasn't much doubt that the Carrera Abarth was purely and simply a racing model. Porsche retained four or five cars for their works racing efforts.

suspension, finned drum brakes and four-cam, twin-plug, flat-four were pure Carrera, dating back five years to the original racing version. Power ranged from 115bhp from the standard 1588cc engine to as much as 185bhp with the ultimate versions of the later 1966cc Carrera 2 engine—delivering more than 140mph. And while Porsche retained four or five cars for the works team, the GTL Abarth was also a customer car, with every example sold before it was built.

For three years it steamrollered everything in the 2-liter GT class. It won its class first time out in the 1960 Targa Florio (finishing sixth overall), the Nürburgring 1000km, Le Mans and Sebring. In 1961 it scored in Sebring, Le Mans, the Targa and the Paris 1000km. In 1962 it completed its Targa and Sebring hat-tricks and became the first GT car to lap the Nürburgring in under ten minutes. It won its GT Championship class in 1961, 1962 and 1963, and even on its final major works appearance, at Daytona in 1963, it took fifth overall. And the winning Porsche with the Italian connection remains a Porsche icon.

Left: The door handles were aerodynamically recessed.

SPECIFICATIONS

Engine Flat-eight, air-cooled
Capacity 1981cc
Bore x stroke 76.0 x 54.6mm
Compression ratio 9.8:1
Power 210bhp
Valve gear Two overhead camshafts per cylinder bank
Fuel system Four twin-choke downdraft Weber 38DCD carburetors
Transmission Six-speed manual
Front suspension Independent, by double wishbones, coil springs, telescopic dampers
Rear suspension Independent, by double wishbones, coil springs, telescopic dampers
Brakes All discs
Wheels Bolt-on, steel/alloy disc
Weight 1410lb. (640kg)
Maximum speed 162mph (260kph)
Production 2 eight-cylinder works cars, 1961–62

718/8 Spyder

In Porsche's museum there is a 718/8 RS Spyder nicknamed "Grandmother." It is one of just two eight-cylinder examples of one of Porsche's greatest competition cars, last of the classic first generation of aluminum-bodied competition Spyders, before plastic bodies became the norm. It was campaigned around the world, on circuits, in long-distance road races and most successfully of all in the European Hillclimb Championship between 1962 and 1964. It marked a major leap in Porsche's commitment to motor sport, a move from production models to cars built specifically for racing, as the sport became ever more specialized and more competitive. For Porsche it was a logical progression.

In 1950 Frankfurt Porsche distributor Walter Glöckler won the German sports car championship in a Porsche-based special with a highly tuned 1100 engine, turned around and mounted ahead of the rear axle, in a tubular frame clothed in a light aluminum body. An open body. Glöckler's Porsche specials repeated their championship wins in 1951 and 1952 with other drivers, and in 1951, in 1500 form, his Spyder set numerous records at Montlhéry, alongside the factory coupes. And Porsche obviously took note of Glöckler's success, because in 1953 they unveiled their own competition Spyder, the 550.

Mainly designed by works engineer Wilhelm Hild, around a simple ladder frame with drum brakes and near-standard suspension, it initially used the new 1500 pushrod engine, giving almost 100bhp on alcohol fuel—and like Glöckler's, the engine was ahead of the rear axle. Also like Glöckler's the open two-seater body was by Frankfurt coachbuilders Weidenhausen, with the option of a coupe type top for races like Le Mans and the Carrera Panamericana.

The first 550 took a debut win at the Nürburgring in May 1953, won the 1500 class at Le Mans in June, and one of two 550s entered in the Carrera won its class there, too. In 1954, further developed with a stiffer chassis, revised suspension, a cleaner shape and Dr Ernst Fuhrmann's new four-cam, twin-plug 1500 engine, they took further class wins in the Mille Miglia and Le Mans. Then the 550 won its class in the Carrera again, driven by Hans Herrmann—in a remarkable third place overall. That win soon brought the Carrera name into the production range, on the four-cam 356 Carrera—and in 1954 the 550S was introduced as a customer competition model. Officially it was the 1500 RS, or RennSport, the Spyder name probably came from Max Hoffman, who imported many examples for racing in America, where they soon became untouchable.

In later 550A form it gained more power, a more complex chassis, further revised suspension and five-speed gearbox—and to satisfy racing rules more than 100 were built, making it commercially important, too. Then in 1958 it gave way to the 718 1500 Spyder, or RSK, with 140bhp and coil spring rear suspension rather than the familiar torsion bars—a car which was also the basis for Porsche's first single-seater racing cars, which took them via the 1960 F2 constructors' championship into a less successful debut in F1.

Above: Engine cooling was of paramount importance with the more highly-stressed racing engines. Porsche paid careful attention to getting as much air in, through louvers in the car's fenders...

Above: The 718/8 Spyder, adopting its flat-eight engine from the early 1960s F1 racing programme, was hugely more successful than the single-seater Porsche racers, competing and winning in everything from endurance racing to the European Hillclimb Championship

Above: ...via the large horizontal engine fan...

Above: ...and out again, through the big open grilles in the tail.

But while F1 results (aside from Porsche's one and only works GP win, by Dan Gurney at Rouen in 1962) were generally mediocre, F1 technology pushed the sports racing cars to another level. New rules for 1960 specified cars to virtually road specification, including taller windscreens, usable luggage space and a functional hood. Porsche developed the RSK into the RS60, then RS61. "Grandmother" continued that classic Spyder line. Built in 1961 with a four-cam four-cylinder engine it took second overall on its debut in the Targa Florio, driven by F1 stars Gurney and Jo Bonnier. But it was in 1962, with a 210bhp 1981cc version of the flat-eight F1 engine, that it really began to dominate—class wins in the Targa Florio and Nürburgring 1000km, second overall in the endurance championship, and a growing list of race and series wins in America.

And then the European Hillclimb Championship, where the four-cylinder models had already won in 1958, 1959, 1960 and 1961 before the 718/8 moved the goalposts again. With F1 taking precedence, Porsche contested few hillclimb rounds in 1962 but in 1963, by which time the 718/8 had the option of a six-speed gearbox and as much as 240bhp, works driver Edgar Barth dominated the championship, and did the same again in 1964. By then, though, "Grandmother" had a daughter joining the racing family, in the shape of the 904.

Above: The strict functionality in the cockpit was combined with a degree of comfort appropriate to long distance racing.

Above: "Grandmother" was one of the last of the "first generation" of Porsche racing Spyders—the first cars Porsche had built from the drawing board purely as racing models.

Above: The headlamps were smoothly faired in behind long perspex covers, while the teardrop-shaped indicators had just enough trim so as not to look totally stark.

Below: This final series was the most aerodynamic to date, but the tubular spaceframe chassis was still bodied in aluminum, where the next racing models would be plastics.

SPECIFICATIONS

Engine Flat-four, air-cooled
Capacity 1966cc
Bore x stroke 92.0 x 74.0mm
Compression ratio 9.8:1
Power 130bhp
Valve gear Two overhead
camshafts per cylinder bank
Fuel system Two twin-choke
downdraft Weber 461DM2
carburetors
Transmission Four-speed
manual
Front suspension Independent,
by trailing arms, transverse
torsion bars, telescopic
dampers, anti-roll bar
Rear suspension Independent,
by swing axle, transverse
torsion bars, telescopic
dampers
Brakes All discs
Wheels Bolt-on, steel disc
Weight c.2060lb. (935kg)
Maximum speed 125mph
(200kph)
Production 126, 1963–64

356C Carrera 2000 Coupe

Above: By the time the 356C appeared, dash-mounted heater controls had changed VW-style knobs for sliding levers.

In the early 1950s, the Carrera Panamericana was one of the fastest, most dangerous, most punishing road races ever devised. Originally celebrating the opening of the Mexican section of the Pan American Highway, it covered more than 2000 miles over several days, on theoretically closed (but not always perfectly policed) public roads, from one side of Mexico to the other. The first running, in 1950, was for stock saloon cars. In 1951 the race was opened up to sports cars, and European specialists like Ferrari, Lancia and Mercedes came to challenge American giants like Lincoln and Oldsmobile for outright victory.

Below: There was a different wheel and hubcap design, prompted by the switch to disc brakes all round, which the 356C had pioneered for production Porsches.

They won, too, at astonishing speeds. In 1953 the winning Lancia averaged more than 138mph for the long final leg, with top speeds nudging 170mph on the public "super-highway." And although Porsche couldn't compete for outright victory, in Mexico as everywhere else they had every chance of taking class wins—which would still have a major effect on Porsche's American sales.

Their first class win came in 1952, courtesy of Prince Metternich in a 356, finishing eighth overall behind the mighty works Mercedes 300SLs. In 1953 the first 1500 pushrod 550 Spyder took first and second in their class while a 356 took the production class again. In 1954 Hans Herrmann took the four-cam 550 to that dominant class win and third overall behind the far more powerful Ferraris of Umberto Maglioli and Phil Hill. And although that was the end of the Panamericana, whose rising death toll had finally become unacceptable, it was the beginning for the Carrera name at the top of the Porsche range.

It debuted on the 356A 1500GS Carrera at the Frankfurt Show in September 1955—brilliantly combining the latest 356 with an only mildly detuned version of the 550's four-cam engine to produce the fastest production Porsche thus far. A limited production car, maybe good for 100 sales maximum, as Porsche first thought—but in reality the start of a whole dynasty.

Above Left: Familiar shapes continued in the nose of the 356C Carrera, with the slightly raked-back headlamps, and in particular the smooth curve of the hood line, showing increasingly distant—but still clearly recognizable—VW Beetle genealogy.

Above Right: Quarter lights had reappeared on the 356B, and continued on the 356Cs.

Above and Right: The overall shape of the 356C cars had barely changed at all from the high-bumper, high-headlight 356B. Carrera wheels used a steel center with an aluminum alloy rim.

Above: The squared-off engine cover shape above the higher bumpers had continued from the 356B, and even if you couldn't read the script, the Carrera was distinguished by its twin tailpipes emerging near the center, rather than below the bumper overriders.

Technically, the engine transplant was easy, and the engine itself was superb. It was designed in 1952 by Dr Ernst Fuhrmann to see how much power could be extracted from the air-cooled flat-four layout—albeit with roller-bearing crankshaft, dry-sump lubrication, two twin-choke downdraft carburetors, and exotic double overhead camshaft heads with bevel gear drive, two plugs per cylinder and inclined valves in hemispherical combustion chambers. In fairness, more or less the only thing it shared with the pushrod production engine was its 1498cc capacity, but when it first ran over Easter 1953 and delivered 112bhp, it demonstrated just what was possible.

It was just the start. In 1954, while it was beginning its racing career, Porsche also put one into Ferry's own 356, then into a 356 Cabrio, and when the 356A offered a chassis with uprated suspension and more rubber on the road, it provided an ideal basis for a production "Carrera."

There were two versions, the fully-trimmed 356A Carrera 1500GS and from 1957 the lighter 1500GT (with plastic windows, alloy bonnet, doors and engine cover, and Spyder front brakes). Both were hand-built and neither very far removed from race engine power, with 110 and 115bhp respectively. They were extremely expensive, very understated save for minimal "Carrera" badging and dual exhausts, but at almost 125mph by far the fastest cars in their class.

During 1958 the Carrera followed the minor body changes of other 356s (as well as offering a very limited production hardtop coupe by Karmann), and capacity was increased to 1588cc in line with the pushrod engines, so although the four-cams reverted to less expensive and more durable plain bearings, power was almost unchanged. What had changed was the production estimate. By late 1959 when the 356B version was introduced at the Frankfurt Show, almost 700 Carreras had been sold—rather more than the expected 100…

It was still growing. Through 1960 and 1961 the 1600 engines saw changes in carburation, lubrication, bearings and ignition (alongside an overdue switch to 12-volt electrics), mainly for reliability. Then at the 1961 Frankfurt Show the 356B-bodied Carrera 2000GS took a far bigger leap, with capacity increased to 1966cc and power to 130bhp, backed by Porsche's first production disc brakes—to go on sale in April 1962 as the Carrera 2, the fastest of all 356 Carreras.

It also had a reputation as being quite challenging to drive, but it survived to the end of the 356 line. That, however, was now looming large.

Engine Flat-four, air-cooled
Capacity 1966cc
Bore x stroke 92.0 x 74.0mm
Compression ratio 9.8:1
Power 195bhp
Valve gear Two overhead camshafts per cylinder bank
Fuel system Two twin-choke downdraft Weber 461DM carburetors
Transmission Five-speed manual
Front suspension Independent, by double wishbones, coil springs, telescopic dampers, anti-roll bar
Rear suspension Independent, by upper and lower radius arms, reversed upper wishbone, lower link, coil springs, telescopic dampers, anti-roll bar
Brakes All discs
Wheels Bolt-on, light-alloy disc
Weight 1540lb. (699kg)
Maximum speed c.160mph (257kph)
Production 120, 1963–64

904 Carrera GTS Coupe

In December 1963 Porsche announced a new car qualifying for the 2-liter GT world championship ranks for 1964 (which required 100 examples to be built). Officially it was the Carrera GTS, to the factory it was the 904, first of a new line of Porsche sports racers. Durability was as important as outright speed, because it was intended for "real long distance races, not artificial sprints." So it wasn't the lightest car in its class but it was one of the strongest, and became by far the most successful. Unique, in fact, in taking back-to-back class wins in the world sports car championship, the Targa Florio outright, a win on handicap in the grueling Tour de France Auto, class wins in the Nürburgring 1000km and Reims 24 Hours, even second overall in a snowbound Monte Carlo Rally—and it was just about usable as a real road car, too.

It was certainly a customer car. Porsche kept the first six for the works team, delivered cars to America in January 1964 and passed the 100 cars required by the rules in April (eventually building 120, including four as spare-part "kits").

While continuing the mid-engined two-seat 550 and 718 theme, it was the first Porsche to use a glassfiber shell bonded onto a relatively simple but hugely stiff and strong fabricated chassis. Suspension followed the coil and wishbone front and four-link rear pattern of Porsche's 1962 F1 cars, beefed up and "productionised" for the heavier sports car and its larger production numbers. The brakes were discs all round, steering used a new ZF rack and pinion with only two turns of lock—which still wasn't always quick enough to catch the notoriously tail happy car if the driver overstepped its nervous limits.

The shell, styled by Ferry's son Ferdinand Alexander (or "Butzi") was in Pantal, a glassfiber, molded for Porsche by Heinkel. Bonded directly to the steel chassis it contributed to the overall stiffness of the structure, but it was difficult to make panels to a consistent minimum thickness, which contributed to the weight problem (early cars could be as much as 160kg over what the rules

Above: The 904 was properly mid-engined, with the flat-four ahead of the gearbox and the line of the rear axle.

Above: Prominent air scoops just behind the doors fed cool air into the engine compartment, and in this case the filler cap is for the dry sump's oil tank. The door catches were push buttons, with space for the pulls neatly recessed into the rear bodywork.

Above: The numerous air intakes that were dotted around the 904 shell varied from car to car—they were largely dictated by the individual car's main racing requirements.

Left & Above: You do not need to look too closely at the very variable panel fits to see that the body builders still had a lot to learn when working in plastic—inconsistent thickness meant the shell was overweight too.

allowed and no 904 was ever pared down to the limit). And it was difficult to make consistently precise shapes—so few 904s had Porsche's usual fit or finish.

The moldings also formed most of the interior, even the seat padding simply slotted into recesses molded into the back wall of the cabin—so the seats weren't adjustable but the pedals and steering column were (and with a choice of seat shapes and sizes available it was actually very comfortable for most drivers, even for endurance racing). It wasn't luxurious, though; with almost zero trim it was fearfully noisy inside, and the token passenger seat was strictly to satisfy racing requirements, with its footwell largely filled by the battery box. The 904 did, however, have reasonable visibility, full instrumentation, and quite a lot of road-legal equipment, from lights to indicators to wipers and washers.

With the originally-planned 911 flat-six not yet available it used a version of the familiar short-stroke four-cam Spyder engine in 1966cc form, which revved like a demon and gave anything from 180 to 195bhp during the brief competitive life of the car. The works dabbled with eight-cylinder versions, but only briefly. And there was a 155bhp "road" version, but it wasn't a big seller!

Below: Although the 904 Carrera was designed primarily as a racing car, it was genuinely roadworthy too—if not very refined

The 904 raced seriously for only two years, dominating its class in both. It won on its debut at Sebring in 1964 (as a prototype before the necessary 100 cars had qualified it as a GT) and in April won the Targa Florio outright. Works eight-cylinder prototypes failed at Le Mans but five four-pots survived, the best in seventh place overall, on the way to winning the 904's first 2-liter GT title. It took that title again in 1965, when Eugen Böhringer also took that highly unlikely Monte Carlo second place, as 215 of the 237 starters didn't even finish.

But as a racing car in an increasingly sophisticated sport, its front-line life was short. The rules changed, and anyway Porsche had learned how to do things better—especially when it came to saving weight and making the car easy to work on. The flat-four generation was also about to be ousted by the flat-six from the new 911—at the beginning of its development rather than the end. So the 904 was superseded by another Porsche Targa Florio winner, the 911-powered 906 Carrera 6, but there were some things the 906 could never repeat from the 904's repertoire. It certainly wasn't a Monte Carlo car.

Left: The 904 brought plastic body panels to Porsche for the first time.

Right: The deeply-recessed rear window made room for a large, flat rear deck and some more engine compartment air intake area.

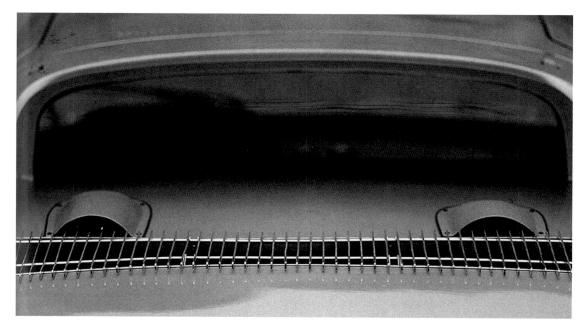

Left: The single, pantograph-type windscreen wiper was a typical bit of minimalist racing design.

SPECIFICATIONS

Engine Flat-six, air-cooled
Capacity 1991cc
Bore x stroke 80.0 x 66.0mm
Compression ratio 9.0:1
Power 130bhp
Valve gear Single overhead camshaft per cylinder bank
Fuel system Six single-choke downdraft Solex 40PI carburetors
Transmission Five-speed manual
Front suspension Independent, by MacPherson struts, lower wishbones, longitudinal torsion bars, telescopic dampers, anti-roll bar
Rear suspension Independent, by semi-trailing arms, transverse torsion bars, telescopic dampers
Brakes All discs
Wheels Bolt-on, steel disc
Weight 2380lb. (1080kg)
Maximum speed 130mph (210kph)
Production 10,723 (including Targas), 1964–67

911 Coupe

Above: A new look for Porsche, after fourteen years of the 356.

I n September 1963 at the Frankfurt Motor Show, Porsche launched a car that would become an icon. It was the successor to the 356 generation, and new in virtually every respect—although still unmistakably a Porsche. If Peugeot hadn't objected to three digits with a central zero it would have been called the 901, which was its project number. But before launch it was redesignated 911.

Ferry called it "a second beginning," and fundamentally it represented his updated interpretation of Porsche's core obsessions—light weight, high power to weight ratio, simplicity where it mattered, and style dictated by function.

The company was in good shape, too. In 1960, for the first time ever, Porsche's turnover had passed 100 million DM, the 356 was still near peak sales performance, the Stuttgart factory had been extended again with its "No 3 works," and a massive new R&D center, test track and advanced design facility was under construction at nearby Weissach. But Porsche, of all companies, knew that standing still could really only mean going backwards.

They had considered several 356-based alternative routes, including four-seater saloons, coupes and cabriolets, designed around

the existing flat-four engine and apparently with only small weight penalties. But Porsche decided to stick with what it knew, so project number 901 would be a sports car, and it would be new from the ground up. It was to outperform even the quickest of 356s, but to be more refined, more comfortable, more practical. Porsche was planning to grow by spreading its appeal beyond the sports car hardcore to a broader audience, but one with more sophisticated expectations.

To Ferry that meant a light, compact 2+2 sports car with a six-cylinder engine behind the driver—six cylinders offering a new development starting point, and not least laying to rest any notion of a Beetle heritage. It was Porsche's first six, and the first entirely-Porsche production engine. They looked at several layouts, starting with a single-central-camshaft pushrod design with air-cooled heads but

oil-cooled barrels for quieter running (one of the key targets for the new engine) but rejected it as too complex. They tried other pushrod layouts with two camshafts, and various carburetor options to improve packaging and maybe create some rear luggage space. But while keeping the planned cylinder dimensions and 1991cc capacity they opted for a single chain-driven overhead camshaft on each cylinder bank, pure air-cooling with a single large fan, light-alloy construction with a vertically-split two-piece crankcase, a seven-bearing crankshaft and two downdraft triple choke carburetors. As launched, it equaled the four-cylinder Carrera's 130bhp best, but had far better refinement, was more economical to build, and easier to maintain.

The car around it was to be roomier but not significantly bigger or heavier, not a full four-seater but a usable 2+2. The shape started as a design exercise from

Below: While still having some of the styling cues of the 356, the new 911 had a more modern, sharper-edged look. Drawn and styled originally by Butzi Porsche, and turned into an engineering design for production by Komenda, it looks as fresh today as it did back in 1963.

Ferry's son Butzi, who had worked with Komenda in the design department since 1957. Komenda, however, charged with turning Butzi's ideas into a production design, was erring towards a larger car and four full seats (which was a personal prejudice)—until Ferry intervened. In decreeing that it would not be a four-seater, would not have a wheelbase longer than 86.5ins. (2.2 meters), would have all torsion bar suspension with front struts and rear semi-trailing arms, all disc brakes, a five-speed gearbox, the previously described engine and room to carry a bag of golf clubs, Ferry defined what the 911 became.

When Komenda anticipated practical difficulties in engineering the style down to size in a unitary shell, Ferry took Butzi's original drawings to Reutter and had them create engineering plans with the style virtually unchanged. They delivered exactly what he asked for: a car with usefully more room inside (including more luggage room), the convenience of wider doors and bigger windows, yet only some 6ins. (15cm) longer than a 356, on a wheelbase only about 5ins. (13cm) longer, and actually slightly narrower than its predecessor.

Right: The simplicity of the 911's styling was of a different generation from that of the 356, but just as striking, and would prove to be just as enduring. In some early cars that front bumper was lead-loaded, to improve the handling balance!

In Frankfurt the yellow show car was well received, the car (now definitively numbered 911) was applauded again when it was ready for independent testing, and generally accepted by the Porsche market even if a few still couldn't see the point in replacing the 356. It didn't actually go into full production until August 1964, by which time it had six single-choke carburetors and a new five-instrument dashboard whose layout would still look familiar to any 911 driver more than 30 years later. But surely, even Porsche couldn't have dreamed that the 911 design would become the icon that it did.

Top to Bottom: Practicality was one of the main themes of the 911's design parameters.

Steel wheels were the original staple option.

The first six-cylinder production engine was as difficult to see as any of the fours had been.

A full-length front hood offered usefully more luggage space and a worthwhile reduction in drag.

As well as the space to carry a full set of golf clubs, that meant a bit more room inside and with better trim and equipment levels—but it was still a sports car.

The flap by the door mirror and radio aerial covers the fuel filler cap, and is released from the dashboard.

SPECIFICATIONS

Engine Flat-four, air-cooled
Capacity 1582cc
Bore x stroke 82.5 x 74.0mm
Compression ratio 9.3:1
Power 90bhp
Valve gear Single central camshaft, pushrods
Fuel system Two twin-choke downdraft Solex 40PJJ4 carburetors
Transmission Four-speed manual (five-speed optional)
Front suspension Independent, by MacPherson struts, lower wishbones, longitudinal torsion bars, telescopic dampers, anti-roll bar
Rear suspension Independent, by semi-trailing arms, transverse torsion bars, telescopic dampers
Brakes All discs
Wheels Bolt-on, steel disc
Weight 2130lb. (966kg)
Maximum speed 115mph (185kph)
Production 30,300 (including Targas), 1965–68

912 Coupe

If the all-new 911 had a deficiency compared with the 356, it was its price. As launched it cost around 30 per cent more than any 356 except the Carrera, a big problem given that one of the 911's tasks was to broaden Porsche's market. It was especially a problem in America, where Car & Driver magazine commented that "at almost $6500, the 911 is more than a Corvette… and within not many dollars of being a mighty expensive car." And although running out remaining stocks of 356s would offer a cheaper alternative for a while, that was neither a long-term nor very satisfactory situation for the newcomer. Porsche needed a compromise, and the compromise was the 912.

In essence, the 912 was a four-cylinder 911. It looked like a 911, it had all the practical advantages of a 911, performance apart it drove very much like a 911, and from Porsche's perspective it was mechanically close enough to the "real" 911 to offer the benefits of cost saving through increased volume, with minimal additional investment. The trick was simply to replace the more expensive bits with less exotic and readily available alternatives. So the 912 evolved as a 911 with slightly simpler trim, a four-speed gearbox as standard, and a four-cylinder pushrod engine carried over from the 356 1600SC.

And there was life in that yet, almost exactly as it left the 356. That meant 1582cc, two twin-choke downdraft carburetors, and

only mildly retuned, to give slightly less peak power (90bhp rather than the 1600SC's 95) but usefully more low- to mid-range flexibility to suit the heavier car.

Otherwise, there were few mechanical differences between 911 and 912. The suspension layout was the same, disc brakes, rack and pinion steering and 12-volt electrics were the same, even a closer ratio five-speed gearbox was an affordable option—and recommended by most testers. With that and the inherent weight saving (both from the engine and the deleted up-market trim), the 912 had ample performance by most standards. Weighing almost 60kg less than a 911 and only about 90kg more than the engine-donor 356, it still offered a top speed of about 115mph—actually faster than the 356 because of better aerodynamics, and only about

Above and Left: There was very little externally to distinguish the 912 from the higher-priced 911, which was exactly as Porsche intended. Steel wheels were standard on the 912, for reasons of cost, but the optional five-spoke alloys offered later gave the 912 even more of a 911 look.

10mph short of the 911. 0-60mph in just over eleven seconds was only about three seconds behind the first 911, it was more economical to run, and as well as being much better than the 356s, with the lighter engine its handling balance was, if anything, better than the early 911s. All that for around 25 per cent less than its six-cylinder cousin, and very little more than the 356SC—which it finally replaced completely during 1965.

Nor was the paring down overdone. A 912 still offered reclining seats, three-speed wipers, heated rear screen, and when the Targa option was introduced on the 911 it was offered on the 912, too. The most noticeable savings were in a simpler, three-dial dashboard and no 911-style wood trim—even the badging was subtle enough not to advertise the difference. And the payoff was that, in 1966, the 912 took two thirds of the new family's sales.

While it lasted, it evolved—a five-dial dash in 1967, echoing most of the 911's chassis changes in 1968, and the options of 911-lookalike alloy wheels, air-conditioning, electric sunroof, tinted glass and so on. But the one area where it couldn't keep up, especially as 911-power started to grow, was in performance. As the gap widened, the 912's days were inevitably becoming numbered.

As several testers pointed out, it wasn't only about numbers, it was about character. What the 911 did easily, the 912 had to struggle for. In 1968 the 911 gained fuel injection, in 1970 capacity was increased to 2.2 liters—by which time the 911 was almost twice as powerful as a 912. It couldn't last. In 1970 the 912 was quietly dropped, although honorably so, because it had more than elegantly served its purpose and it had a following all its own.

There was one final twist. In 1976 the 912 made a brief and low-key reappearance in the one-year-only 912E. The formula was familiar—a 911-based car with less elaborate trim and lower-cost power. This time, though, the power didn't come from the car that had preceded the 912 but the one that had replaced it, when it was originally dropped in 1970. That was the very different 914, a mid-engined sub-911-level car built in partnership with VW—and as it turned out, further proof that the 911 was a hard act to live up to.

Below Right: The real difference between the 912 and the 911 was below the familiar tail, where lurked the 1.6-liter flat-four engine from the last of the 356s, rather than the 2-liter flat-six from the first of the 911s. A four-speed gearbox was standard, but five speeds were a popular option.

Below Left: The nose of the 912 was identical, even down to retaining the bumper overriders, which some manufacturers might have dropped to save money.

Below: The elegant lines of the 911 came as standard, even in this cut-price sibling.

Below: With shared bodyshells, the 912 naturally retained neat 911 features like the flip-up filler flap in the front fender, which was released from inside the car by a simple knob on the dash.

Below: The slant of the headlamps, the neat air intake grilles and the combined turn indicator and parking light units were all pure 911.

SPECIFICATIONS

Engine Flat-six, air-cooled
Capacity 1991cc
Bore x stroke 80.0 x 66.0mm
Compression ratio 8.6:1
Power 110bhp
Valve gear Single overhead camshaft per cylinder bank
Fuel system Two triple-choke downdraft Weber 40IDT PI carburetors
Transmission Five-speed manual (four-speed Sportmatic optional)
Front suspension Independent, by MacPherson struts, lower wishbones, longitudinal torsion bars, telescopic dampers
Rear suspension Independent, by semi-trailing arms, coil springs and auxilary rubber springs, telescopic dampers
Brakes All discs, ventilated fronts
Wheels Bolt-on, steel disc (light-alloy discs optional)
Weight 2110lb. (957kg)
Maximum speed c.125mph (200kph)
Production 3350, 1969–72

914, 914/6

Above: Without the Targa bar, the 914—in spite of its mid-engined layout—would have looked almost ordinary, but Porsche didn't get to be Porsche by following the herd.

With 911 sales flourishing, competition glory piling up, and lucrative outside design and development contracts aplenty, Porsche were doing well by the late 1960s. But they had ambitions to do even better. They still needed a bigger seller, a car in the old 912 mould to fill the gap below the 911.

The 912 had worked as a cut-price 911-clone, now Porsche envisaged a low-cost, high-volume car with a personality totally separate from the 911s. For the first time, a distinct second line. If they had a problem, it wasn't designing such a project, it was funding it so soon after the hugely expensive 911 launch, and finding space to build it in the numbers needed to fulfil its purpose.

The key was Porsche's relationship with VW and the final catalyst was that VW were seeing almost the same problem from the opposite direction—they had massive volume but wanted a car with a sporty personality to add prestige to the VW badge. It looked almost a perfect match. The idea of a joint venture sports car, capable of wearing either Porsche or VW badges depending on specification, price and market, had reached its time.

The partnership evolved as a flexible affair—in effect a "gentleman's agreement" between Ferry Porsche and VW boss Heinrich Nordhoff. As originally conceived, it would see VW commission Porsche to create a high-profile VW sports car based around the 1.7-liter fuel-injected flat-four of their 411 saloon, which with six-cylinder power could also be a high-volume Porsche.

Combining their legendary design skills with almost unrestricted access to the VW parts-bin, Porsche planned a mid-engined layout, as in the one-off 356-1, as opposed to a rear-engined one as in the 356 and 911. And if 356-1 plus the mid-engined competition cars from 550 to 908 (and most recently the mighty 917) hadn't already done so, that should finally have disproved any notion that Porsche stuck to the rear-engine layout more out of stubbornness than science.

To many people, a bigger issue was how the new car would look. Butzi was credited with the final shape and detail, but it had started as a study for a front-engined BMW sports car, by industrial design agency Gugelot. It was hard to call it pretty, but it was certainly of its time,

Below: The 914's styling started life on a front-engined BMW project, but was heavily revised by Butzi Porsche.

Left: The car's Targa-type roll-over hoop created a new and admirably versatile roof style, which soon found its way onto other Porsche models.

Middle Left: The badging acknowledged Porsche's role in the project.

Below Left: The mid-engined layout raised a few eyebrows among hard-core Porsche fans.

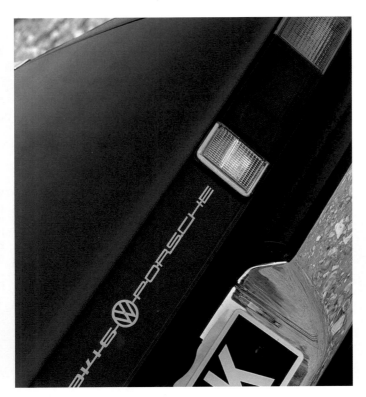

Below The five-spoked alloy wheels on the 914/6 were one of the stronger Porsche hallmarks.

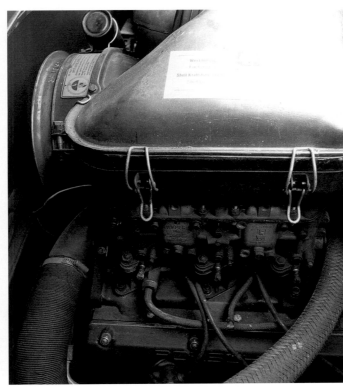

and functional. It was low, wide, with a long-wheelbase, short overhangs even with mandatory American oversize bumpers, the first pop-up headlamps ever seen on a Porsche, and a removable Targa top between the steeply sloping windscreen and large roll-hoop around the rear window. To sum up how different the proportions were, it was 7ins. (177mm) shorter overall than a 911, but the wheelbase was 7ins. (177mm) longer.

Practicality was important, especially with an eye to the planned VW market. It was strictly a two-seater, but roomy, and (thanks to the low-set mid-engine) offered generous luggage space front and rear—the downside being more difficult access to the engine for routine servicing.

The flat, air-cooled choices began with VW's iron-barreled, alloy-headed, fuel-injected, 1679cc, center-cam

Below: The 914 was both versatile and impressively practical.

Left: The big bumpers were dictated by the need to be saleable in the U.S.A. with minimal changes, and pop-up headlights were used for the first time on a Porsche.

Far left: The interior was fine for two—but no more.

pushrod four, giving a modest 85bhp but with strong torque from remarkably low speeds. The six was straight out of the 911T, immediately before that car switched to 2.2 liters. So, 1991cc with two triple choke Weber carburetors, 125bhp, and plenty of flexibility of its own. Enough, in fact, in a car that would have weighed almost 242.5lbs. (110kg) less than a 911, to have embarrassed the 911T had it not increased its own capacity.

The 914 was unveiled late in 1969, with four-cylinder sales promised almost immediately and the 914/6 for 1970, but the 914 family was already in trouble. Nordhoff had been succeeded at VW by Kurt Lotz, and the loose partnership had changed significantly, notably in establishing a joint sales company, with 50/50 ownership. Worse, the supply arrangement had changed. Lotz had

decided that VW stood to make more from selling fully-trimmed shells (as opposed to bare ones) to Porsche than they did from selling what, on the VW scale, would actually be a very small volume of the VW version.

It changed everything. The 914 remained reasonably cheap and sold reasonably well, though never to the once-anticipated 30,000 a year scale. The expensive 914/6 bombed, selling only 3360 cars before being dropped in 1972, and a purely-Porsche 190bhp 2.4 916 project was stillborn. Two years later Porsche bought out VW's distribution interests, but although the 914 passed 100,000 total sales, another new generation of VW management was already eyeing another direction, featuring a water-cooled, front-engined car. In 1976, still just short of 120,000 sales, the 914 was dropped, too.

SPECIFICATIONS

Engine Flat-six, air-cooled
Capacity 2687cc
Bore x stroke 90.0 x 70.4mm
Compression ratio 8.5:1
Power 210bhp
Valve gear Single overhead camshaft per cylinder bank
Fuel system Bosch mechanical injections
Transmission Five-speed manual
Front suspension Independent, by MacPherson struts, lower wishbones, longitudinal torsion bars, telescopic dampers, anti-roll bar
Rear suspension Independent, by semi-trailing arms, transverse torsion bars, telescopic dampers, anti-roll bar
Brakes All ventilated discs
Wheels Bolt-on, light-alloy
Weight 2115lb. (960kg) (lightweight version)
Maximum speed c.150mph (240kph)
Production 1580, 1972–73 (all models)

911 Carrera RS 2.7

Above: The rear rim widths were increased for the RS, and the wheelarches were subtly flared to accommodate them, with the rear bumper and skirt neatly following suit. The engine cover was in glassfiber.

Below: The return of one of the great model names; when Porsche recreated the Carrera, they weren't afraid to shout about it.

It took Porsche a long time to put the evocative "Carrera" badge onto a 911—more than seven years from the car's launch. But when the first 911 Carrera appeared, it was a car worthy of the name—the 911 Carrera RS 2.7.

To Porsche, Carrera meant "outstanding performance and appearance." The RS 2.7 had both, and a racing role, as the foundation for almost a quarter-century of all-conquering 911 racing derivatives, including the 1979 Le Mans-winning Kremer K3 version of the Group 5 935, and even the 1996 winner, the GT1 prototype, still with recognizable 911 genes. In 1972, the RS 2.7's role was to qualify the 911 for its category in the world sports car manufacturers' championship, which required a minimum production of 500 cars. That was too small a number to justify a totally bespoke design and build program, too big for a car which could only be a racer, or too expensive for potential customers. In fact it was a good rule, which created a generation of racing sports cars which were fast and competitive, but which had genuine production roots, and were viable enough as road cars to justify the numbers demanded.

In late 1972 a 911 was 2.4 liters, the stroke having been lengthened late in 1971. While increasing power for Europe, more capacity preserved it for America—with other modifications to meet increasingly stringent emissions regulations. The most potent European 911S could thus offer up to 190bhp, but for racing Porsche needed even more. To do that, they needed to go beyond 2.5 liters while staying inside the 3-liter limit—which wasn't in itself a problem as the furthest the 911 six would stretch without a complete redesign was 2.7 liters. What was a problem was that other manufacturers could get much closer to the limit, so Porsche had to perform their other specialty, "adding lightness."

Off the shelf, the 2.7 RS offered 210bhp, a modest increase, and was offered in a "touring" spec with most of the 911's standard creature comforts. The production lightweight version, however, used thinner steel in the shell, molded glassfiber for the engine cover, thinner glass, little or no heat or sound insulation, no rear seats, and much lighter, thinly-padded racing seats in front. What didn't have to be there wasn't, and for anyone who did mean to go racing there was the even lighter RSR—stripped to the bone, with aluminum door and bonnet skins. Quoted weight for the "touring" was 2286lbs. (1037kg), for a "production" RS lightweight 2116lbs. (960kg), and for the very focussed RSR, as little as 1984lbs. (900kg).

There was a bonus. Porsche not only met the 500-car Group 4 production requirement, but an astonishing total sale of 1580 cars in 1973 also qualified the 2.7 RS for the less exotic Group 3 category, which gave the

opposition a very big problem indeed. They had sold 1331 "touring," 200 "lightweights," and 49 RSRs, which were in effect off-the-shelf Group 4 racers, including more power.

For the 1973 championship, 2.8 liters, twin-plug heads and new camshafts gave 300 and eventually, once capacity had reached a full 3 liters, up to 330bhp. From launch, the lightweight road car was already Germany's fastest production car, with a 150mph max and 0–60mph in the five-second bracket. A full-race RSR would deliver 170mph and 60mph in less than four seconds—figures few seriously quick cars could approach even thirty years later...

Beyond big power and light weight, the distinctive five-spoke alloy wheels put wider rubber on the road at the back, five speeds were standard where four were still familiar on many 911s, suspension had stiffer springs, thicker anti-roll bars and gas dampers, and ventilated disc brakes gave the lighter cars astonishing stopping power, even without the usual assistance.

Visibly, the RS sprouted wider rear arches, the distinctive "Carrera" stripe graphics on the flanks and large Porsche script on the tail—and the famous "ducktail" spoiler made its first appearance on the engine cover. By later standards it is modest, in 1973 it was sensational, but it was also functional, reducing tail-lift by almost 198lbs. (90kg) at maximum speed, and improving the handling by moving key aerodynamic forces back by a significant amount. Not least, the ducktail gave the RS an instant nickname, which stuck through other models.

Thirty years on, the Carrera 2.7 RS and its relations appear even more as cars way before their time. For the violent intensity of their acceleration and the sheer power of their braking in particular, they set standards that are impressive even now, and made almost any contemporary look feeble. They were the start of an unrivalled racing dynasty, and of the real rise of the 911 towards true supercar status. And of course, they were worthy Carreras.

Above: The five-spoke alloy wheels were color-coded to the Carrera script, and all in arrestingly bright colors.

Above Right: Not every spoiler from every manufacturer since has been so honest, but the RS's "ducktail" had a truely functional role.

Above: A five-speed gearbox was standard RS wear.

924

Engine In-line four-cylinder, water-cooled
Capacity 1984cc
Bore x stroke 86.5 x 84.4mm
Compression ratio 9.3:1
Power 125bhp
Valve gear Single overhead camshaft
Fuel system Bosch K-Jetronic injection
Transmission Four-speed manual
Front suspension Independent, by MacPherson struts, lower wishbones, coil springs, telescopic dampers, (anti-roll bar optional)
Rear suspension Independent, by semi-trailing arms, torsion bars, telescopic dampers, (anti-roll bar optional)
Brakes Discs front, drums rear
Wheels Bolt-on, steel discs (light-alloy optional)
Weight 2260lb. (1025kg)
Maximum speed c.125mph (200kph)
Production 150,951, 1976–85

When it came to offering a lower-priced, higher-volume alternative to the 911, the 924, after the 912 and 914, proved to be third time lucky. Yet it might have looked the least likely of those three to succeed. It was certainly the furthest removed from what most assumed made a Porsche a Porsche. It had a water-cooled engine in the front, rather anonymous styling, and originally it wasn't even supposed to be a VW, let alone a Porsche. It should have been an Audi, after Audi had joined the VW group in the mid-1960s.

And in a way it was more logical for VW to try to launch a sports car with the sportier Audi badge than a VW one as they'd intended with the 914. It was also logical now for VW to opt for a water-cooled engine, because new VWs like the Golf would, and it was time to start distancing modern VW from the Beetle.

VW had already dabbled with and rejected a mid-engined 914 successor based on a planned water-cooled flat-four Beetle replacement, because that car itself was rejected in favor of the front-engined, front-drive Golf. And new generations of VW management had ended the marketing partnership with Porsche. But in 1970, VW's latest boss, Rudolf Leiding, commissioned Porsche to create an Audi sports car from the Audi and VW parts-bins—a comfortable, easy to drive 2+2 with the space and practicality of a 911, but for the masses.

Politics and practicality suggested the water-cooled front engine—Audi's 2-liter injected four, with modern, belt-driven overhead camshaft. With a choice of available transmissions, including front-drive, the layout was left to Porsche, but before any firm decisions were made, VW cancelled the whole project, much to Porsche's annoyance. They had done a lot of work, and been paid for it, but the real money would have been in the joint production arrangement, plus a new shared platform for a high-volume Porsche. So Porsche bought the project back from VW, reportedly for 160 million DM—or something close to their design fee. The car would continue to use Audi and VW parts, and be built by Audi in Neckarsulm, but it would become a Porsche, and called 924.

Once it was completed, that was. Fortuitously, it benefited (technically and in terms of image) from being developed alongside another front-engined Porsche, the 928—not least in adopting a similar layout of front-engine, rear-transaxle linked by a rigid torque tube, for almost perfect weight distribution. The shape, by Dutchman Harm Lagaay, was bland, but with bigger wheels and modest spoilers, the later 924 Carrera would show it didn't have to be. It was a viable 2+2, simply trimmed to keep costs down, but comfortable, and the shape was effective—as launched in 1975 its 0.36Cd was standard-setting.

They used the parts-bin skillfully, so although the Audi engine wasn't exotic it was effective, and with Porsche's aluminum cylinder head and Bosch injection it gave 125bhp. The rear-mounted transaxle gearbox was originally a four-speed manual (with three-speed automatic option), but from 1977 a five-speed manual was optional, and eventually it became standard. Front suspension used MacPherson struts (ex-Beetle) and lower A-arms (ex-Golf), the rear had

Above Left: Even with the chunkier wheels, the 924 Turbo kept the smooth, slightly weak flanks of the normal 924—the bigger-arched look only appeared on the more extreme Carrera GT.

Beetle semi-trailing arms and Porsche transverse torsion bars. To keep basic prices low, anti-roll bars and alloy wheels were only options, brakes were front (Audi) discs, rear (VW) drums, and rack and pinion steering was Golf—like much switchgear and minor trim. It was a well conceived package, which worked. It wasn't refined but it was quite quick, managing around 125mph and 0–60mph in 10.5 seconds. The handling was exceptional, with big grip, great

Above Middle: The 924 was first developed for VW and was to be badged as an Audi, but after VW pulled out Porsche bought the project back.

Above Right: The interior of the 924 was steadily improved, but it never completely reached refined, even when the car had become a lot more expensive.

Above: As launched in 1975, the 924's slippery shape set new standards for low drag, and the Turbo took performance to 140mph levels.

balance and a forgiving nature—compromised by a notoriously rough and noisy ride.

Although it was expensive (and apparently out of Porsche character), it was successful, soon accounting for sixty per cent of Porsche sales. Over the years, ride problems were addressed, equipment levels improved, and from 1978 there was a seriously quick version, the 170bhp, 140mph Turbo, which got even quicker in 1980, with

177bhp. Even that was eclipsed by the 210bhp, 150mph 924 Carrera GT, with more aggressive looks and uprated suspension, transmission and brakes. Much of which reflected another cousin—the 944, which gave the 924 a detuned version of its 2.5-liter four-cylinder Porsche engine in 1985 to create the 924S, but then started to steal the 924's sales to the extent that the original car was retired in 1988. But it had been good while it lasted.

Top Left: The fatter alloy wheels of the Turbo gave the 924 some of the image that had been lacking in the basic car, and turbocharging gave it a much more impressive performance.

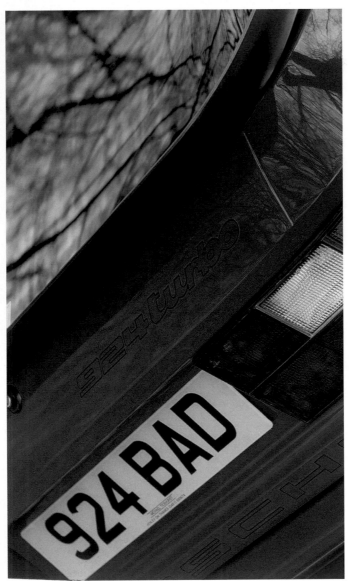

Bottom Left: The tail end didn't quite achieve the simplicity of the 911, but that was part of the penalty of cutting costs via the parts bin— and the hatchback was useful.

Above: In many ways the 924 looked very much like the 944 that was about to follow. The lattice-style wheels were an attractive option—at an extra cost, of course.

Left: With turbocharging, power output of the four-cylinder engine leapt immediately to 170bhp—with a bit more to come.

SPECIFICATIONS

Engine Flat-six, air-cooled
Capacity 2857cc (3999cc with 1.4 x turbo equivalency formula)
Bore x stroke 92.8 x 70.4mm
Compression ratio 6.5:1
Power 590bhp
Valve gear Single overhead camshaft per cylinder bank
Fuel system Bosch mechanical injection, two KKK turbochargers
Transmission Four-speed manual
Front suspension Independent, by MacPherson struts, lower wishbones, coil springs, telescopic dampers, anti-roll bar
Rear suspension Independent, by semi-trailing arms, coil springs, telescopic dampers, driver-adjustable anti-roll bar
Brakes All ventilated discs, with adjustable front/rear balance
Wheels Center-lock, light-alloy
Weight 2138lb. (970kg)
Maximum speed 212mph (340kph)
Production 2 works cars, 1976; 13 similar customer cars, 1977

935 Coupe

Motor racing rule makers are often criticized, but occasionally they are the catalyst for something great. And, through sports car racing rules which have required at least an element of production-based technology (and a minimum production requirement), that has included many Porsches.

In 1976 the World Championship for Makes was to new Group 5 rules—production based cars with strictly controlled modifications and a minimum production run, in this case defined by the fact that a Group 5 car also had to be homologated for one of the lesser Groups. It didn't require any further "production" run, and extensive further modification was allowed, but the rules did at least create a generation of genuinely production-based cars.

Broadly, Group 5 limited minimum weight and maximum tire width (both related to capacity), and aerodynamic add-ons. A number of basics also had to be retained from the lesser model—including major engine components, the suspension layout (but not the details), engine position, and most of the shell.

Porsche's starting point was the 911 Turbo, or 930 (unveiled in production form at the 1974 Paris Show) and its racing cousin the RSR Turbo. From which evolved the Group 5 935—in its day the ultimate evolution of the classic 911. While still clearly 911-based, in its most extreme form the 935 delivered up to 850bhp and close to 220mph. In 1976 it put Porsche back on top of the

Makes series. In private hands it continued to dominate into the 1980s—and in 1979 it was an outright Le Mans winner for the Kremer team.

Porsche had created the 930 specifically as a stepping stone through Group 4 (and a minimum of 400 cars) to Group 5, and stepped back from racing in 1975 to concentrate on development. The 1976 weight limit for a 4-liter Group 5 car (or under equivalency rules, a turbocharged 2856cc one like the 935) was announced as 2138lbs. (970kg). To reach that, Porsche had to put 154lbs. (70kg) of ballast back, so successful had they been with the 930's diet. That had removed insulation, rust-proofing, trim, and all bar the driver's seat (now on a titanium frame). All glass save the windscreen and driver's side window was replaced with Perspex; door skins, bonnet, engine cover and huge new wheel arches were glassfiber. As well as the huge rear wing, a deep-skirted flat nose with recessed headlamps gave vital downforce. And the advantage of ballast over ordinary weight was that, after much testing, Porsche could distribute it to improve handling balance—as well as putting things like the battery, extinguisher and oil and fuel tanks in the nose, to balance the mandatory rear engine location.

Right: Somewhere under all the aerodynamic addenda that kept it on the ground and the sponsorship messages that kept it on the championship trail, the 935 coupe retained the unmistakable 911 shape.

Below: Contrary to appearances, Group 5 regulations limited the size of aerodynamic devices—such as the high rear wing and downforce-producing wheelarches—but the signwriting emphasized them anyway.

As required, crankcase, cylinder barrels and crankshaft were essentially standard 930. Almost everything else, from camshafts, to lubrication system, to manifolding, to Bosch mechanical injection (even vertical rather than horizontal cooling fan), was new. So was the 2856cc capacity—within a thimbleful of the maximum allowed for a turbo engine and arrived at by reducing the bore of the 3-liter production engine slightly but with identical stroke.

Originally they used one large turbocharger and an air-cooled intercooler in the vast rear spoiler. When the rule-makers objected to that layout they compromised with smaller, but heavier, water-cooled intercoolers. That was mitigated by a starting point of almost 600bhp, and enough flexibility to allow a four-speed gearbox—based on the standard 930 unit which had been designed to withstand this far more extreme application. Huge ventilated and cross-drilled disc brakes with four-piston calipers were derived from the mighty 917 racer, while suspension retained the production layout (as required) but with ultra-light titanium coil springs and cockpit adjustable roll settings.

Despite political and development hiccups, the works 935 took the 1976 World Championship of Makes, before customer 935s took over, while Porsche themselves concentrated on winning Le Mans outright with the 936 prototype. Twin turbos made the 935 more powerful and more responsive, helping win the 1977 title, with further "privateer" wins right through to 1981. And for 1978, Porsche had created the most extreme of all 935s, "Moby Dick."

Under the long, low, wide, mainly white bodywork (liberally interpreting the rules) "Moby Dick" had a 3210cc capacity—taking it above the 4-liter class and imposing a heavier 2260lbs. (1025kg) weight limit—water-cooled, four-cam, four-valve heads, 845bhp and a maximum beyond 220mph. It raced only twice, and won once (at Silverstone)—but at Le Mans its thirst restricted it to eighth overall.

A 935 did win Le Mans, though, and a private one, at that. In 1979, as a mediocre Group 6 challenge faltered, the Kremer 935 K3 of Klaus Ludwig and Don and Bill Whittington won, ahead of the 935 of Rolf Stommelen, Dick Barbour and movie icon Paul Newman. But the real star that day was the 935.

Below: Stripped to basics, the single-seat cockpit was still recognizably 911-derived. The angled rev-counter sets the red-line at vertical, in common racing practice.

Below: The car shown here is the 935 "baby," an even lighter version of the Group 5 car with a 370bhp 1.4-liter flat-six turbo engine.

Below: The rear wing was there to keep the car on the ground—and to carry the all-important sponsor's message.

Below: To save weight, the door skins, hood, engine cover and huge new wheelarches were all in glassfiber.

SPECIFICATIONS

Engine Flat-six, air-cooled
Capacity 3299cc
Bore x stroke 97.0 x 74.4mm
Compression ratio 7.0:1
Power 300bhp
Valve gear Single overhead camshaft per cylinder bank
Fuel system Bosch K-Jetronic injection, single KKK turbocharger
Transmission Four-speed manual
Front suspension Independent, by MacPherson struts, lower wishbones, longitudinal torsion bars, telescopic dampers, anti-roll bar
Rear suspension Independent, by semi-trailing arms, transverse torsion bars, telescopic dampers, anti-roll bar
Brakes All ventilated discs
Wheels Bolt-on, light-alloy
Weight 2940lb. (1335kg)
Maximum speed c.160mph (257kph)
Production 22,542, 1978–89

911 Turbo (930)

In 1974 the 911 made the leap from sports car to supercar, in the 930—or 911 Turbo. 260bhp, 155mph, and 0–60mph in less than six seconds made it one of the fastest road cars in the world. Unsurprisingly, there was a racing motive too.

The Turbo, like the four-cam Carrera engine, was conceived by Professor Ernst Fuhrmann, who in 1972 had moved from the design office to run the restructured company. As with many Porsche creations, it was a convincing illustration of the old adage that racing improves the breed—although for once, Porsche weren't pioneering the technology, only following others.

In fact turbocharging as a means of increasing power had been patented in 1905, and was fairly common on diesel truck engines since the 1950s. In essence it is simply supercharging, but with the compressor driven by exhaust gases rather than mechanically from the engine. In its commercial diesel application, space for packaging wasn't a problem, exhaust temperatures were far lower than for a petrol engine so less of a problem for the hardware, and "turbo-lag" (a lack of instantaneous throttle response) wasn't an issue. For any engine, turbocharging increases power without any loss from a mechanical drive. And the

gains are potentially huge, which was why designers worked hard to adopt turbocharging for petrol engines, especially for racing cars and high-performance road cars. The drawbacks are a need for careful packaging and exotic, heat-tolerant materials, and that inevitable throttle-lag, but by the time Porsche opted for turbocharging for the 930, the problems were being solved.

Turbocharging had long been used in American oval racing, where maximum power was more important than instant response, and Porsche had already used it for their massively powerful CanAm versions of the racing 917—producing more than 1000bhp from 5.4 liters. Porsche also saw its potential for the new Group 5 sports car racing category in Europe, and a turbocharged production 911 was an essential starting point for a turbocharged Group 5 car—both technically and to satisfy the minimum production required by the rules.

Porsche began work on a turbocharged 2.7 road car in 1973, and showed a wide-wheeled, big-winged (but non-running) study in Paris in September. In 1974 they built their first turbocharged, Carrera RSR-based, 911 racer—in fact a testbed for the planned production car, and nominally a 3-liter (from 2142cc multiplied by the 1.4 "equivalency" factor applied to turbo engines). With one big turbocharger it gave more than 500bhp in qualifying trim, and encouraged Porsche to persevere with the road car even though the Arab-Israeli war was threatening fuel crises, and the whole image of high performance cars.

Far Left: The massive rear wing helped with both downforce and cooling.

Left: Porsche were far from reticent in emphasizing the 911 Turbo's competition connections, either in the exaggerated body bulges and heavy-duty aerodynamic add-ons, or in the sponsor's colors, as used on some limited edition cars.

Below: The visual changes from any "ordinary" 911 were no more than any hot-rodder might have done, but the effect was spectacularly aggressive.

AAH 379X

Above: The power generated by the turbocharged engine required a good deal more rubber on the road.

Above: It may have been visually not much more spectacular than any other hidden-from-view 911 engine installation, but the flat-six engine with single turbocharger was hugely more powerful.

Right: This view really was the only one that any other car normally saw!

Above: Turbo power and torque required only four gears on the floor, but demanded some big numbers on the dashboard.

Left: The Turbo was a fine example of racing lessons being carried over for the road, something Porsche had learned to do far better than any other manufacturer.

So the luxurious, expensive, super-fast production 911 Turbo was previewed at the 1974 Paris Show, without compromises. The single-turbo 3-liter flat-six produced 260bhp, with massive mid-range flexibility, and enough off-boost power to guarantee that turbo-lag wasn't a big problem. It only needed four gears, and almost everything else was uprated: clutch, brakes (with ventilated RS Carrera discs), wheel and tire size, rear hubs and suspension arms—and bodywork, with wide arches and the big rear wing.

Production proper started in 1975 and Porsche soon passed the racing homologation figure of 400 cars. In 1978 capacity was increased to 3.3 liters (by increasing both bore and stroke) and power to 300bhp. An air-to-air intercooler made the turbocharging more effective by keeping the temperature of the intake air down and its density up, compression ratio was increased and the bearings were uprated—all to guarantee reliability while increasing power. The brakes were modified to keep pace with the power, using cross-drilled discs and four-pot calipers, fed back to the road car from the 935 racing derivative—and in turn derived from the legendary 917 Le Mans prototype racers.

For the roadgoing 911 Turbo, the changes weren't only aimed at outright power and performance but at driveability and refinement—and not least at meeting the new generation of environmentally conscious regulations that were gathering momentum after the energy crises of the mid 1970s. Having said that, it didn't change too many more times for the rest of the model's life—which took it to the end of the 1980s. In 1983 Porsche managed to find slightly more torque with much better fuel consumption, but the last major change came in 1986 with another power and performance leap. A bigger turbocharger, bigger intercooler and new exhaust system lifted power to 330bhp, top speed to more than 170mph and shaved the 0–60mph time ever closer to five seconds dead. And that was how the first generation 911 Turbo continued—until 1989.

SPECIFICATIONS

928S

Engine 90° V8, water-cooled
Capacity 4644cc
Bore x stroke 97.0 x 78.9mm
Compression ratio 10.0:1
Power 300bhp
Valve gear Single overhead camshaft per cylinder bank
Fuel system Bosch K-Jetronic injection
Transmission Five-speed manual (four-speed automatic optional)
Front suspension Independent, by upper wishbones, lower trailing arms, coil springs, telescopic dampers, anti-roll bar
Rear suspension Independent, by multi-link Weissach axle, with upper transverse links, lower trailing arms, coil springs, telescopic dampers, anti-roll bar
Brakes All ventilated discs, ABS anti-lock system
Wheels Bolt-on, light-alloy
Weight 3420lb. (1550kg)
Maximum speed c.155mph (250kph)
Production 10,205,1979–83

O f all Porsches, the 928 is one of the most misunderstood and underestimated—dismissed by Porsche Luddites because it didn't fit their idea of the air-cooled rear-engined "norm," underestimated by its doubters because they couldn't accept that it was actually a very good Porsche indeed.

Porsche themselves were less jaundiced. By the early 1970s they had seen a wider market beyond the hardcore sports car driver, for Porsche performance and dynamics with greater refinement and comfort, in true Grand Touring style. Development chief Helmuth Bott had even suggested a layout to fit the profile—water-cooled, front-engined, with lazy reserves of power. It would be quieter, roomier, more easily able to meet increasingly stringent emissions and safety requirements. But it would handle and perform like a Porsche.

It was a time of change: the company itself had been restructured, VW's new regime had pulled the plug on a Porsche-designed Beetle replacement—and with it the planned high-volume replacement for the only partly successful 914/6, below the 911. But while the 924 would eventually bridge that gap, the 928 would emerge as a Porsche at the far end of the scale.

Dr Fuhrmann, now managing director, gave the go-ahead in October 1971 (on his birthday), after the board had rejected alternatives including a large mid-engined car (too difficult to provide enough space) and a full four-seater (too close to a saloon, and out of Porsche character). In fact they followed the old Porsche mantra, "cobbler stick to your last." So Project 928 would be the biggest Porsche so far—on a wheelbase 8.5ins. (22cm) longer than a 911's—but essentially still a sports car; a two-door 2+2 GT, with large capacity, front-mounted,

water cooled V8 linked by a torque tube to the rear-mounted transaxle gearbox, for optimum weight distribution, fine handling and comfortable ride.

Development proper started in November 1971, envisaging a compact, highly refined, low-maintenance, short-stroke, single overhead-camshaft, all-alloy V8, of around 5 liters and 300bhp. The initially troublesome torque-tube chassis layout was refined with a stronger propshaft (running at engine speed, because the gearbox wasn't in unit with the engine) in uprated bearings, while mounting the gear-linkage on the torque tube reduced noise and vibration.

Engine development had its hiccups, too. The first two prototypes, in January and March 1971, both broke on test, before the third (with injection, as planned for production) worked. Meanwhile, the chassis and transmissions (a choice of five-speed manual or three-speed Daimler-Benz automatic) were being developed on test cars variously disguised as Audis, Opels or Mercedes. By late 1973 they had progressed to endurance testing of an almost complete 928 chassis disguised by a widened Audi coupe shell, before the project was almost abandoned in the face of threats of an energy crisis. That hit Porsche anyway, and would have been even worse for a bigger, thirstier car like the 928, so the project was temporarily put into low gear—until Porsche bit the bullet.

In November 1974, scrapping contingency plans for a four-seater or a 911-engined 928-clone, the 928 was re-confirmed,

Left: Molded side strakes first appeared on the 928S, to break up the visually over-heavy slab sides of the original 928.

Left: Some fourteen years before the 968 was launched, the 928 set a new, softer family style, carried through in this 928S

with a small reduction in capacity (to 4.5 liters) and a bigger drop in power (to 240bhp). But there was a superb chassis, with coil-sprung multi-link "Weissach" rear axle, clothed in a softly-rounded shape designed in-house by Tony Lapine. It was aggressively broad shouldered, with distinctive integral, polyurethane-skinned bumpers and pop-up headlights and, naturally, it was controversial. But soon after it was launched at the Geneva Show in March 1977 it was dubbed International Car of the Year.

It wasn't perfect. The cut in power, in quite a heavy car, hurt the 928 more than Porsche would have liked, and there were lesser problems with minor details and with road noise. Characteristically, Porsche responded with a revised version, in 1979. As the 928S it clawed back a lot of the earlier compromises. Capacity increased to 4.7 liters, power was back to 300bhp, it had better brakes—and by 1982 it had ousted the base 928 completely, having been uprated again. With uprated injection it climbed to 310bhp, and with a four-speed automatic option and "second generation" ABS it evolved into the 928S2.

There was never an S3, but in 1985 emissions-conscious America got a 5-liter, four-cam, four-valve V8 which was soon adopted for other markets. That delivered 320bhp and in mid-1986, the 928 reached 928S4 form—a subtly more aggressive looking car promising almost 170mph and all the true GT character the 928 had ever aspired to. In 1989, 340bhp took the 928S4GT beyond 170mph, and in 1991 the 928GTS, with 5.4 liters, 350bhp and even more performance, finally took the 928 almost beyond criticism—for those who understood.

Above: The flip-up front lights and the smooth lines of the pillars and mirrors were designed to cut down wind resistance.

Right: The big, front-engined car had a different sort of presence from the 911.

Right: The integral bumpers were clad in a knock-absorbing polyurethane skin.

Right: The center console reflected luxury aspirations, with an on-board computer, air conditioning and top-class entertainment.

Far Right: Die-hards might believe that a Porsche should be rear-engined—but the badge clearly indicates that Porsche themselves did not agree.

Left: Everything about the 928's shape was designed to appeal to the eye—and to cheat the wind.

911 Carrera 3.2

By the early 1980s, nearing its twentieth birthday, the 911 should by any normal reckoning have been long retired. Instead, in 1984, it was reborn. It had never stopped evolving, but this wasn't just another model change, it was virtually the start of a new generation. There was a new engine, new transmission, bigger brakes, and suspension and body changes. And since 1983 there had been one more body style beyond the familiar Coupes and Targas—a full Cabriolet. All of which suggested that Porsche had no plans to lose the 911 yet a while.

Far from being rendered obsolete by the 928, it was selling as strongly as ever, and Porsche's 250,000th car, built in June 1977, had been a 911. New boss (and 928 creator) Dr Fuhrmann had less of a personal relationship with the 911 than Ferry Porsche had, but Fuhrmann's next creation, the 944, launched in 1981, hadn't killed it either. Basically, the market wouldn't let it go.

The appearance of the 928 and 944 had one downside for the 911, it had led to a period when the 911 wasn't upgraded quite as diligently as it usually was, perhaps because Fuhrmann in particular assumed that it was about to disappear anyway. But in that respect at least, he was very, very wrong.

To date it had progressed through 2 liters to 2.2, 2.4, 2.7 and most recently to 3 liters, as much to reconcile power, economy and driveability with more restrictive emissions regulations as simply to increase power outright—although that happened as well. The body had evolved with regulations, too, notably with higher bumpers from 1974, which (rather than take the easy way out and tack-on enough to get by) Porsche redesigned properly, to suit both new American demands and a more aesthetically demanding world market.

Equipment levels had been continuously upgraded, especially in "comfort" areas such as heating and ventilation (which to be fair was originally quite crude), until the 911 was now a performance car you could live with. It was more user-friendly dynamically, too. Ongoing development, from lead-loaded front bumpers on the first cars to a longer wheelbase in 1968 (in each case to improve weight distribution), to ever wider wheels, tires and tracks, to regular improvements in brakes and suspension details, had tamed (if not totally eradicated) its early waywardness, especially at the back. So twenty years on, far from showing its age, it had rarely been better—but it had slipped a little.

Above Top Left: Five-spoke wheels were still a Porsche trademark.

Above Bottom Left: Door mirrors were big but neat, and were electronically adjustable.

Above Top Right: Laid-back lights had for a long time had lenses molded to shape, and now they could have washers too.

Above Bottom Right: The whale-tail spoiler looked dramatic, but the louvers did not feed the intercooler, as on the Turbo.

Right: Far from being killed off by the 928, the 911 tightened its grip on the affections of Porsche aficionados with the long running Carrera 3.2.

By the end of the 1970s, the 911 was down to two basic models, the 300bhp Turbo and 3-liter 911SC which replaced the Carrera. And as Fuhrmann concentrated on other projects, they had stagnated slightly. But come 1981 Fuhrmann had retired and new chairman Peter Schutz (an American) had put the emphasis back on the 911. The Cabriolet (a design exercise in Frankfurt in 1981 but in production for 1983) was one manifestation; all-wheel drive for the Cabrio and the 959 supercar were further signs that the 911 had a future under Schutz. The reappearance of the Carrera name for 1984 simply confirmed it.

Nominally 80 per cent new, the 3164cc flat-six combined a longer-stroke Turbo crankshaft with the latest alloy block, bigger valves, higher compression, new manifolding and new digital management—to increase power to 231bhp while being more economical than the SC that it replaced. The gearbox had new ratios and its own oil cooler, brakes were uprated again, and Carrera buyers could also specify Turbo-style winged bodywork and big wheels—plus the Turbo's uprated suspension and cross-drilled brakes. Everything except Turbo power, in fact, for considerably less money. Which kept 911 sales nicely buoyant, in spite of recession, until the Carrera 2 arrived in 1988.

If there was a worry, it was that (partly due to Schutz's influence) Porsche had become unhealthily

dependent on America, which took some 62 per cent of sales by 1987, and that they had committed themselves to expansion, which looked less sustainable as world markets wobbled. When they did wobble, at the end of the 1980s and into the 1990s, both sales and profits slipped badly. But confounding predictions, Porsche hung on in. Schutz had invested wisely in research and development facilities, and R&D contracts covered shrinkage in car sales. Perhaps most of all, Schutz was indisputably the man who had saved the 911 with the introduction of the new Carrera for 1984. And whatever was happening to other iconic sports cars, people were still buying them.

Left: By the 1980s, the whale-tail spoiler had pretty much become a 911 trademark, but it did serve a practical purpose in improving rear-end stability at the sort of speeds the 911 had become capable of.

Below: When the Carrera 3.2 was "reborn" in 1984, it had more power, and better handling and styling, which evoked the best of the Turbo look.

SPECIFICATIONS

Engine In-line four-cylinder, water-cooled, twin balancer shafts
Capacity 2479cc
Bore x stroke 100.0 x 78.9mm
Compression ratio 8.0:1
Power 220bhp
Valve gear Single overhead camshaft
Fuel system Bosch Motronic management, single KKK turbocharger
Transmission Five-speed manual
Front suspension Independent, by MacPherson struts, lower wishbones, coil springs, telescopic dampers, anti-roll bar
Rear suspension Independent, by semi-trailing arms, transverse torsion bars, telescopic dampers, anti-roll bar
Brakes All ventilated discs
Wheels Bolt-on, light-alloy
Weight 2975lb. (1350kg)
Maximum speed c.155mph (250kph)
Production 18,161,1985–91

944 Turbo

The 944 was unveiled at the Frankfurt Show in September 1981, and finally gave Porsche reason to believe that they had at last plugged the sub-911 void. It was clearly related to the 924, and rather suggested that the 924 itself hadn't been too far short of filling the troublesome gap. What had been wrong, it now transpired, had been curable. The wide-wheeled wide-arched and be-spoilered 924 Carrera GT had shown that a bit more visual muscle could transform the 924's slightly bland and narrow-shouldered look; and the 924 Turbo had shown that the chassis wasn't fazed by considerably more power. On which evidence, a 924 sibling with real Porsche power was a car just waiting to happen.

Porsche already knew that, but didn't have the right engine. They had been working on one, though, and it would be entirely Porsche. Not a flat-six, and not a V6 or small V8, either, which had both been considered and rejected as adding unnecessary complication to the range. So Porsche went for what

seemed an unlikely alternative, a large capacity in-line four, initially naturally-aspirated but with options for long-term development in many directions.

A four would fit with few problems under the bonnet of a 924-based shell, wouldn't conflict with current thinking on economy and emissions control, and would be able to draw extensively on the basic thinking of the 928 V8. On the downside, refinement could be a problem with a big, thumping four, but that was the sort of challenge that Porsche were happy to rise to.

The 944 engine, however, evolved as considerably more than half a 928 V8. A 2.5 four obviously had reference points in a 5-liter V8

(including bore spacing and valve layout), but very few parts would be shareable. And in one respect the four would be more sophisticated than the V8—with twin contra-rotating balancer shafts to smooth out the inherent imbalance of four big cylinders.

Otherwise the single-overhead camshaft, eight-valve fuel-injected and electronically-managed all-aluminum engine was quite conventional, and offered 163bhp with a wide and flat torque curve. It was inclined by 30 degrees to keep the low bonnet line, and used fluid-filled mountings, further to reduce any vibrations transmitted to the shell. The shell itself, while essentially 924, had wider arches (on part of the main steel shell, not tacked on glassfiber parts as on the Carrera), wider wheels, and

generally a more muscular character. The superbly balanced torque-tube chassis and identical suspension layout were retained, with ventilated disc brakes all round and the usual choice of five-speed Audi manual or three-speed VW automatic transmission. Even the interior was virtually identical, if a little better trimmed and equipped.

Launched in 1982, the 944 was a winner. It was quick (at 135mph), refined, handled brilliantly, and it was keenly priced—at least in the early days. And the happy result was that from the start it became the fastest selling Porsche ever. As normal, Porsche continuously developed it. There was a new dashboard in 1985 and a smaller, height-adjustable steering wheel. Then later that year, there was a major power boost and a new model, in the 944 Turbo.

Left: The 994 had really strong styling—it was nothing like the rather bland 924 from which it had evolved.

It was no longer expected to replace the 911 but the 2.5 four, plus turbocharger and intercooler, was potent—with 220bhp, five-speed manual transmission, and no auto option. Suspension was uprated with alloy rather than pressed steel arms and new transaxle mounts, there was a larger molded fuel tank, and from 1987 standard ABS, which soon filtered down to other 944s.

In 1986 Porsche offered a twin-cam, 16-valve head (echoing 928 changes), better breathing, higher compression and power up to 190bhp, pushing top speed to over 140mph—in the 944S. From 1988 there was a Turbo S, initially as a 1000-off special edition, then as a 250bhp production model—and luxury options now included such things as air-conditioning, electric windows, central locking, power steering and electrically height adjustable driver's seat.

The entry-level eight-valve 944 leapt to 2.7 liters in 1989, improving both power and flexibility; and in the S2 the 16-valve S was taken to almost 3 liters and 210bhp, with most of the Turbo's running gear. The S2 offered the option of a cabriolet, but as it was the only topless 944 it was apparent that the range was soon to go. The 2.7 eight-valve went first, then the Turbo Coupe and both versions of the S2. And late in 1991, the 944 was replaced by the 968—which was similar enough in concept to suggest that the 944 had done its job well.

Above: The square-jawed nose of the 944 Turbo is so strongly proportioned and detailed that it looks right even with the headlights popped—and that is a rare achievement for any car.

Left: The Turbo badge also signified handling—and stopping—improvements.

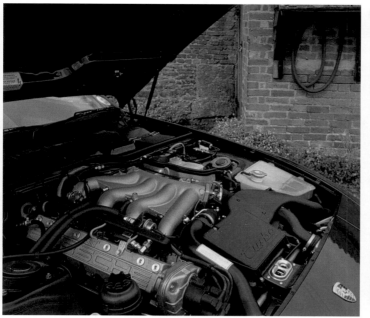

Above: A more sophisticated engine than appearances suggest, with twin balancer shafts to soften the thud of four big cylinders, and a water-cooled turbocharger to liberate lots of power.

Above: The interior trim may have looked rather odd at first, with the subtly-strong stripes on the upholstery, but it quickly grew on you. The Turbo also finally offered a better steering wheel position.

Above: By any standards, the 944 is a purposeful looking car. The stubby tail looks hugely better for a neat spoiler.

959

Engine Flat-six, air-cooled
cylinders, water-cooled heads
Capacity 2849cc
Bore x stroke 95.0 x 67.0mm
Compression ratio 8.3:1
Power 450bhp
Valve gear Two overhead
camshafts per cylinder bank
Fuel system Bosch DME
management, twin KKK
turbochargers
Transmission Six-speed manual,
variable-split four-wheel drive
Front suspension Independent,
by double wishbones, coil
springs, twin telescopic
dampers, anti-roll bar
Rear suspension Independent,
by double wishbones, coil
springs, twin telescopic
dampers, anti-roll bar (front
and rear have height and
damper adjustment on
some models)
Brakes All ventilated discs,
ABS anti-lock system
Wheels Center-lock, light-alloy
Weight 2977lb. (1350kg)
(Sport version)
Maximum speed 197mph
(316kph)
Production 250,1987–88

Right: The 959 was the most
technically advanced supercar to
date, but it also came in a
uniquely user-friendly package.
Hugely expensive and built in
limited numbers, it was a car to
be savored by a lucky few.

Below: The four-wheel-drive, near 200mph 959 was
once the most extreme roadgoing Porsche of them all,
but below the aerodynamic add-ons, its relationship to
the 911 is unmistakable, especially in the distinctive
roof line.

The mid-1980s was an age of booming economies and spectacular supercars. Porsche's was the expensive and strictly limited production 959—the most technically advanced road car thus far seen, and one of the fastest. It looked very like a 911 with a rather exotic body kit, and of course it was 911-based, but complex and effective chassis technology (including electronically controlled four-wheel drive and driver-adjustable suspension) made this near 200mph 911-clone a uniquely user-friendly package which still has few peers.

Originally it was intended as another race and rally homologation car for the new Group B, which allowed extensive technical freedom but demanded a minimum "production" run of 200 identical cars—too many to be sold only as competition cars, so implying a genuine road-car connection. And for rallying, where Group B was king, that also created cars like the 288GTO from Ferrari, the Sport Quattro from Audi and the RS200 by Ford, but none matched the 959.

Right Top: Providing adequate cooling was one of the major problems during the 959's evolution, and the rear fender scoops channel cool air to the engine.

Right Bottom: Even the compact external mirrors on the 959 paid ultimate homage to aerodynamics.

It debuted in Frankfurt in 1983 as the Gruppe B design study, and exactly twenty years after the 911 itself was launched there was no doubting the Gruppe B's starting point. A low-drag body, mainly in composites, clothed most of the 911's central monocoque. The flat-six engine was still behind the gearbox, and although it had water-cooled, four-valve, twin-cam cylinder heads and twin turbochargers it was firmly rooted in the 956-type production six. Capacity was increased from 2.6 to 2.8 liters and with low boost settings, 400bhp was way inside the engine's potential, favoring durability and driveability.

The rest was considerably more exotic. Brakes and suspension were 911 race-car based, while the transmission featured a six-speed gearbox plus complex, electronically-controlled four-wheel drive, with viscous center-coupling and driver-controllable torque-split for varying conditions. Porsche planned to build the necessary 200 cars in time to go racing in 1985, but even for Porsche that was a tough target—which, for once, they failed to hit.

In 1984, as development continued, the Gruppe B became the 959. It gained bigger wheels with tire-deflation sensors, additional cooling vents in the nose and tail, adjustable ride-height and damper settings, more responsive turbos and even more sophisticated transmission specifications. With simpler four-wheel drive and 3-liter engines (detuned to a modest 225bhp for reliability on questionable quality fuel) three examples ran in the 1984 Paris-Dakar Rally—and René Metzge's Gruppe B/959 hybrid won outright.

But sheer complexity, additional features (and not least strikes in the German motor industry) delaying the start of production for the 959, initially from 1984 to April 1985. At that time, projected prices were announced, at a massive DM420,000 even for the road version (which would account for the bulk of production) and DM650,000 for the 961 competition model—but it would still be some time before you could buy either. And there were setbacks. In 1985 none of the three 230bhp 959 prototypes entered in the Paris-Dakar finished—with two eliminated by accidents and the third by oil-pump failure.

And as the 959's schedule slipped, its raison d'être was about to disappear altogether. By 1985 the rally cars that Group B had created had become 500bhp monsters which brought near GP car performance to the forests. At the end of 1986, after a series of tragic accidents involving both competitors and (worse) spectators, Group B was outlawed as too dangerous.

Porsche still hadn't started 959 production, but now they couldn't afford not to—if only in road car form to recoup some of their massive investment. It finally happened in 1987, when the 959, all problems resolved, became the world's fastest production car. Now it had a 2.85-liter four-cam, four-valve flat-six with water-cooled heads and turbochargers, titanium conrods and two intercoolers. Electronic boost control made it reasonably docile at low speeds, and with the second turbocharger blowing through the first, colossally powerful at higher speeds—peaking with 450bhp and 369lb. ft. of torque.

Porsche offered two versions, the slightly lighter and more basic Sport and the fully equipped Comfort. Both had the driver-selectable four-wheel drive modes and continuously variable automatic torque split for optimum traction; both had height- and stiffness-adjustable, self-leveling suspension and massive, ABS-equipped brakes. Comfort versions had leather and air-conditioning, too, but would already leave any other car on the road for dead. The Sport offered 197mph, 0–60mph in 3.7 seconds and 0–100mph in a staggering 8.3 seconds—and achieved in deceptive ease thanks to the 959's unrivalled technical sophistication. And that, as much as performance alone, was what defined this world-beating Porsche supercar. Colossal, exploitable performance backed by extraordinary refinement and usability, even in marginal weather and road conditions. Racer or not, there was simply nothing like the 959.

Far Left: The interior would have felt familiar to any 911 owner, save for a six-speed gear change, and additional switches and instruments for variable four-wheel drive and suspension systems.

Left: The tightly-packed engine bay. The ducts behind the rear wheels (see below) are sited just aft of the twin turbo intercoolers.

Below: If anything, the sculpted sills emphasize rather than disguise the added width of the 959's composite bodywork.

SPECIFICATIONS

Engine Flat-six, air-cooled
Capacity 3600cc
Bore x stroke 100.0 x 76.4mm
Compression ratio 11.3:1
Power 250bhp
Valve gear Two overhead camshafts per cylinder bank
Fuel system Bosch DME management
Transmission Five-speed manual (Tiptronic automatic optional)
Front suspension Independent, by MacPherson struts, lower wishbones, coil springs, telescopic dampers, anti-roll bar
Rear suspension Independent, by semi-training arms, coil springs, telescopic dampers, anti-roll bar
Brakes All ventilated discs, ABS anti-lock system
Wheels Bolt-on, light-alloy
Weight 3040lb. (1380kg)
Maximum speed c.160mph (257kph)
Production 1989-1993

911 Carrera 2 & 4

It was neither a secret nor an exaggeration to say that early 911s handled differently to most high-performance sports cars. Their rear-engined weight bias undeniably gave a tail-wagging tendency if you overstepped the limits, and you needed a degree of skill to get it back. It was all part of the character of the car. But over the years, perhaps Porsche's greatest achievement was to refine the 911's manners without losing the best parts of that unique personality.

Not that they abandoned their core philosophy, only developed it. So even as the 911 aspired to front-to-rear balance, the big masses at either end ensured that once you'd overstepped the mark, the car still behaved like a rotating dumbbell. And if the driver lifted off the power while cornering hard, the tail, by dint of pure physics, did have an inclination to overtake the nose. But Porsche knew as well as anybody that that could intimidate "ordinary" drivers, so they did work hard to let development triumph over design—continuously. In fact they had already started that process with the 356, tuning weight distribution and suspension detail alike to calm its

on-limit nerves. And from the start, they followed the same path with the similar layout of the 911...

Year on year, model on model, modification on modification, testers acknowledged what Porsche was achieving, until in December 1989 Autocar summed up the progress to date. "The 26-year amelioration of the 911's handling deficiencies," they said, "reached its apogee with the Carrera 4, which, through sheer weight of technology, crushed tail slides precipitated merely by lifting off the throttle mid-bend out of existence. That the Carrera 2 displays a similar disinclination to let go at the back is even more impressive, especially since it is paired with a sense of agility and adjustability seldom apparent in the C4... "

Like many others, they reckoned the Carrera 2 "the best 911 yet." The 4's four-wheel drive apart, Carreras 2 and 4 shared the same new suspension, the same new engine, the same beautifully understated new shape with its smoothly integrated front and rear bumpers and subtle, pop-up rear wing. And although Porsche reckoned this 911 was 85 per cent new, it was still 100 per cent 911.

Capacity reached 3.6 liters, with new crankcase, crank, rods, pistons, twin-plug heads with twin distributors, revised inlet and exhaust plumbing, and the very latest Bosch Motronic electronic engine management. With 250bhp it became the most powerful naturally aspirated 911 production engine to date. Yet with almost twice the power of the first 911, it had far better manners. It still had struts and lower wishbones at the front, semi-trailing arms at the rear, but now it adopted coil springs all-round, as well as ABS brakes. And for the first time outside the lofty world of the 959, the new family offered four-wheel drive, with variable torque split, in the ground breaking Carrera 4.

It offered a nominal torque split of 31/69 per cent front/rear, with a version of the 959's electronically-locking PSK differential system to vary that split according to conditions, in hundredths of a second—and in theory with the ability to send up to 100 per cent of the drive to either end. It also offered an automatic gearbox, the 911's first since 1979, and a sophisticated one at that. Based on the PDK double-clutch system of the 962C endurance racer (and jointly developed with Bosch and ZF), Tiptronic offered both fully automatic or clutchless manual changes, with

Below Left: The styling of this Carrera harks back to the simplicity of the earliest 911s, but it is neatly updated with strong "family" details, like the integrated nose and tail moldings, which were pioneered by the 928S.

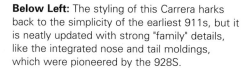

Top: The center tunnel is deeper to allow for four-wheel-drive parts, but the Carrera interior is basically familiar save for the long-absent option of an automatic gearchange.

Middle Left: The retractable tail spoiler that Porsche developed for the Carrera 2 & 4 was a neat element of the cars' back-to-basics smoothness.

Middle Right: A tell-tale for this excellent Tiptronic auto appears in the speedo.

Bottom: The engine bay is visually no more exciting than it ever was, and the flat-six is now also largely encapsulated from below for better sound deadening, but with twin-plug heads and capacity up to 3.6-liters, this was the most powerful normally aspirated 911 engine of all.

"intelligent" shift programs. Its gate featured both a "conventional" PRND32 auto and a +/- position for one-touch clutchless-manual up and down shifts. There was lots of development to come, with more ratios and even more refined and sophisticated shift programs. But from the start, far from being a slow and dull, "lazy-driver's" self-shifter, Tiptronic was genuinely sporty, allowing full-power up or down shifts without even lifting off the throttle—all backed up by clever electronics to prevent any inappropriate shift which could damage either engine or handling balance.

It was just one more feature on a brilliant new generation of 911. These new Carreras, both rear- and four-wheel drive, were almost universally reckoned to be the most competent yet, with greater refinement again, and the most user-friendly handling so far. But of course, there had to be a catch. Finally, the same testers who had once criticized the 911's nervousness now wondered if it had perhaps grown a bit too friendly, too clinical. No change there, then.

Left: The heater controls are much simplified from older models, but the Carrera interior is basically familiar.

Above: The retractable rear spoiler flips up at open road speeds and disappears neatly at town speeds, and it helps cooling as well as aerodynamics.

Below: When it first appeared, the Carrera was hailed as the most competent 911 ever, with great refinement and handling that had finally become almost idiot-proof.

SPECIFICATIONS

Engine Flat-six, air-cooled
Capacity 3299cc
Bore x stroke 97.0 x 74.0mm
Compression ratio 7.0:1
Power 320bhp
Valve gear Single overhead camshaft per cylinder bank
Fuel system Bosch K-Jetronic injection, single KKK turbocharger
Transmission Five-speed manual
Front suspension Independent, by MacPherson struts, lower wishbones, coil springs, telescopic dampers, anti-roll bar
Rear suspension Independent, by semi-training arms, coil springs, telescopic dampers, anti-roll bar
Brakes All ventilated discs, ABS anti-lock system
Wheels Bolt-on, light-alloy
Weight 3218lb. (1460kg)
Maximum speed c.170mph (273kph)
Production 4107, 1991

911 Turbo

The 1991 911 Turbo reflected both turbulent times and Porsche's progress. A replacement for the previous generation Turbo with all the best genes of the new Carreras, 2 and 4, it had been conceived while economies were booming and any Porsche was the car of choice for the Yuppie aristocracy. That made this the most powerful, the most sophisticated, and by far the most expensive Turbo to date. But by the time it was unveiled, in Geneva in 1990, the Yuppie boom was beginning to bust and environmental conscience was growing. For once, it looked as though Porsche, in an attempt to capitalize on a market which was about to collapse, had been caught out.

In a new age of cynicism, reviewers even questioned whether the new Turbo was different enough for surviving buyers, or extreme enough. "It looked," said Autocar, "like a mellow 959… but there was a general feeling that Zuffenhausen should have waited a year… then it would have featured the new six-speed manual gearbox and a four-valve version of the 3.6-liter Carrera 2 engine with another 50 or so bhp. In the face of supercar activity from Lamborghini and Ferrari and the coming Bugatti, Jaguar XJ220 and Mercedes C112, the Turbo is no longer the supercar standard setter… "

But the new Turbo was another Porsche to defy logic. In the short break after the previous Turbo ended production, extensive modification (including new manifolding, a bigger turbo and intercooler, a more efficient wastegate and revised electronic management) had hiked the two-cam, two-valve 3.3 Turbo's output to 320bhp, while catalysts had reduced emissions, and a "double mass" flywheel from the new 3.6 Carreras had reduced both noise and vibration. And if some people were disappointed that it still only had five gears instead of six, they needn't have worried—332lb. ft. of torque meant that was all it needed.

While it missed out on the new Carrera four-cam, four-valve architecture, it did adopt the new generation's coil-spring suspension in place of torsion bars—in this more potent car with stronger rear arms to cope with the added power and more rubber on the road, plus stiffer springs, dampers and anti-roll bars. New geometry also introduced a small amount of passive rear-steer action, in another tweak to pacify the inevitable tendency to lift-off oversteer.

The Turbo, too, was shifting subtly towards more user-friendly character. The interior detail hadn't changed much, but for the first time, a Turbo offered power steering, ABS on even bigger ventilated and cross-drilled discs with four-piston calipers, and more grip from wider rubber on larger diameter five-spoke alloy wheels (which were big enough to distinguish the Turbo at a glance, even from the latest Carreras). It looked more aggressive, too, with its deeper front and rear bumper-airdams, neat, low sills, wider wheel arches, and the big, old-style "picnic-table" fixed wing (incorporating the intercooler) rather than the new Carrera family's smaller and more discreet pop-up type.

Post-959, it put the Turbo back at the top of the range in performance terms, and kept Porsche head to head with its "production" supercar rivals. It would nudge 170mph, hit 60mph in less than five seconds, 100mph from rest in less than 11.5 seconds, and 120mph in under 17 seconds. But for once there was more to its personality than performance alone. Or perhaps less…

The consensus was that while the new Turbo was massively fast

(given its head), had a brilliant chassis, staggeringly effective brakes, impressive steering feel and feedback even with its new power assistance, and had plenty of old-style 911 flat-six aural character, it also had its shortcomings. It wasn't as refined as it might be, but far worse, it wasn't as immediate. The big new turbocharger had promised better responses but didn't deliver them—in fact from low speeds in high gears it had brought back the old demon, turbo-lag. It made the new Turbo more demanding to drive quickly, and by being less responsive it squandered some of the gains of the brilliant new chassis. And there were smaller irritations. The wider, lower-profile tires and stiffer suspension settings, while undoubtedly enhancing control, introduced a degree of harshness in the ride, and a level of road noise on poor surfaces, that other 911s had long left behind. Oddly, in developing in a direction that was supposed to make the Turbo less uncompromising, it had created compromises in the core character of the car. Which begged the obvious question—had the ultimate 911 finally revealed the classic model's outer limits?

Left: The Turbo was further distinguished from its less potent siblings by the new and rather 959-like alloy wheels and smaller, more aerodynamic door mirrors.

Below: Although it generally follows the smooth-bumpered, deep-silled look of the Carrera 2 & 4 models from which its chassis is derived, the 1991 911 Turbo also had the familiar Turbo styling themes of oversize wheel arches and the big, fixed "picnic-table" spoiler.

Above: The Turbo engine had a bigger KKK turbocharger and intercooler and also gained a "double-mass" flywheel from the new 3.6 engines, which improved both noise and vibration dampening.

Above: One thing different on the dashboard layout is the numbers—a 180mph speedometer is not fanciful for a 170mph car.

Below: There is no mistaking the classic 911 roof and window line, but some testers found its performance disappointing on everyday roads.

Left: The interior might be rather more luxurious and elaborate than that of the earlier 911s, but it is recognizably related.

Right: The cross-drilled and ventilated brakes now featured ABS as well as the usual four-pot callipers.

SPECIFICATIONS

Engine Flat-six, air-cooled
Capacity 3600cc
Bore x stroke 100.0 x 76.4mm
Compression ratio 11.3:1
Power 260bhp
Valve gear Single overhead camshaft per cylinder bank
Fuel system Bosch Motronic management
Transmission Five-speed manual
Front suspension Independent, by MacPherson struts, lower wishbones, coil springs, telescopic dampers, anti-roll bar
Rear suspension Independent, by semi-training arms, coil springs, telescopic dampers, anti-roll bar
Brakes All ventilated discs, ABS anti-lock system
Wheels Bolt-on, light-alloy
Weight 2634lb. (1195kg)
Maximum speed c.160mph (257kph)
Production 2364

911 Carrera RS

In some ways, with the 1991 Carrera RS Porsche moved forwards by looking backwards—creating more by including less. In September 1990 they welcomed back the evocative RS badge with the line, "Rebirth of a Legend"—the legend being the ducktailed Carrera RS 2.7 and 3.0 of the early 1970s. And the near twenty-year gap between RSs showed Porsche didn't use the badge lightly. To them, it was "exclusively reserved for a lighter and more powerful version of a given model." Which was precisely what the new RS would be.

The starting point this time was the latest Carrera 2, and as a generation of racing 911s evolved from the original RS homologation cars, the new RS evolved from a racing version of the latest Carrera—the ones from the 911 Carrera Cup series, a European one-model championship, introduced in 1990, for Carreras with strictly limited modifications. For racing, a small increase in power, a bigger decrease in weight, revised suspension and brakes, all aimed at driveability, safety, and maximum competitiveness between similar cars. For the road, much of the same, for the kind of driver Porsche knew would accept rather less comfort and refinement for rather more performance and excitement—a balance some thought the new Carrera had changed.

So the new RS road car took the Carrera 2 and added lightness. It junked comfort options like electric windows, mirrors and seat adjustment, the central locking, alarm system, sunroof, air-conditioning and power steering, the rear seats, most of the sound insulation, and all the in-car sound system. Instead, it had a carpeted rear luggage shelf, and racing-style solid-shelled front bucket seats, lacking back-rake adjustment, but giving very positive location. Then fully-trimmed door panels were replaced with simple flat moldings, with no oddment pockets, manual window winders and nylon-loop door pulls. And all that added up to a claimed weight saving of about ten per cent—bringing the RS close to 2712lbs. (1230kg) as opposed to the Carrera 2's weightier 2998lbs. (1360kg).

On the "more" side, the four-cam, two-valve, twin-plug 3.6 flat-six was only mildly modified (mainly in engine management) to give a modest increase in power and torque, from 250 to 260bhp and 228 to 240lb. ft., with a greater emphasis on mid-range flexibility and across-the-board responsiveness. Together, weight saving and power hike raised power-to-weight ratio from 188 to 216bhp per ton, and that alone was enough to change the whole

character of the car. What changed it even more, though, was the chassis modifications, which were again focused on performance and involvement, not really on comfort.

It sat wider and lower, on 17-inch RS Cup style five-spoke magnesium alloy wheels, whose 7.5- and 9-inch front and rear rim widths would allow the RS to race in Group N/GT production sports car classes—because Porsche planned to build the necessary 1000 copies of the RS by the end of 1991 to

qualify it for that series (and once again, they handsomely beat that projected output).

It wasn't for everybody. Race-type ultra-low-profile, asymmetric-tread Yokohama tires offered loads of grip and steering feedback but very little ride comfort. And like the suspension set-up (lowered, with stiffer springs and dampers) they gave a nervous feel on anything but a super-smooth surface. Front brakes used the Turbo's bigger, ventilated, cross-drilled discs and the rears were from the Carrera Cup cars—a most effective combination for both stopping power and feel, confirming the RS's

Above: Minimalism was the order of the day for the RS interior, with the simplest of trim, deletion of almost all the electrically-operated options like windows, seats and mirrors, and even the radio. The racing style seats are flamboyantly trimmed but offer quite superb location at speed.

Below: The more aerodynamic wing mirrors are borrowed from the 911 Turbo. The wheels are Turbo style, with the rim size fixed by racing needs and the open pattern giving better cooling for uprated brakes.

personality as a racing car that could be used on the road as much as a road car that could go racing.

Visually, though, subtlety reigned, inside and out. Bright color options and wide, low proportions apart, it was simply a Carrera. And inside, it looked and felt for all the world like an old-style 911, characterized as much by what wasn't there as by what was. Not quite Spartan, definitely functional.

Dynamically, too, it was pure old-style 911. Straight-line performance wasn't hugely different, with a max of 160mph and 0–60mph shaved to around 5.3 seconds, but the RS feel bore little relation to the bare figures. It felt, and sounded, alive—as raw sounding as the finest early 911, and as responsive. In all respects, throttle, steering, brakes, super-crisp gearshift, and pure balance. On a poor surface it could leap and dart alarmingly, on a good one it was the epitome of 911 sharpness brought right up to date. If the Turbo felt dull through the wheel, the RS felt razor-sharp, and impeccably balanced, almost totally free of understeer and roll and crying out to be driven to its limits. Which all added up to a car entirely worthy of one of Porsche's most famous badges.

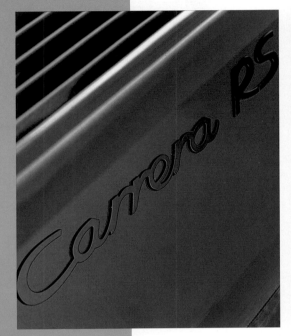 

Above Left: It took Porsche a long time to put the RS script back on the engine cover of a Carrera; the initials stand for Renn Sport, and this production model was based on the Carrera 2 as modified for the one-model Carrera Cup race series.

Above Right: The flat-six was only mildly modified, but its character changed markedly. The jump from 250bhp to 260bhp, and from 228 to 240lb. of torque at 4800rpm, combined with the weight saving, lifted the 188bhp per ton to a highly respectable 216, which changed the whole feel of the car.

Right: The smooth-nosed body styling of the new RS was essentially identical to the normal Carrera 2 & 4 models, but the lowered ride-height in particular gives a more aggressive look.

Right: Porsche resisted the temptation to fit the big, fixed, Turbo-style rear spoiler to the RS and settled for the neat retractable spoiler from the Carrera 2 & 4. With the spoiler down, the RS's tail is as uncluttered as on any 1960's 911 model.

SPECIFICATIONS

Engine In-line four-cylinder,
water-cooled, twin balancer
shafts
Capacity 2990cc
Bore x stroke 104.0 x 88.0mm
Compression ratio 11.0:1
Power 240bhp
Valve gear Two overhead
camshafts, four valves
per cylinder
Fuel system Bosch Motronic
multi-point injection
Transmission Six-speed manual
(Tiptronic automatic optional)
Front suspension Independent,
by MacPherson struts, lower
wishbones, coil springs,
telescopic dampers,
anti-roll bar
Rear suspension Independent,
by semi-training arms,
transverse torsion bars,
telescopic dampers,
anti-roll bar
Brakes All ventilated discs,
ABS anti-lock system
Wheels Bolt-on, light-alloy
Weight 3020lb. (1370kg)
Maximum speed c.155mph
(250kph)
Production 11,245, May
1992–95

968

With the 944, Porsche had finally filled the sub-911 gap with a winner. At its peak it accounted for more than half of Porsche sales, at over 20,000 cars a year. It was respected for its fine chassis and decent performance, especially in the 211bhp S2 and 250bhp Turbo. There was even the Cabriolet option. But the 944 never quite escaped the "bigger 924" connotations. And as time passed, it grew worryingly detached from its low-priced roots. By the late 1980s, with sales falling, it was time to rethink the 944 equation again.

Porsche's options were change it or drop it. Possibilities included a "high-performance estate," a Speedster, a Cabrio-shaped hardtop, and (predictably) higher performance variants, from a slightly quicker GT to a truly rapid hybrid using the 928's 5-liter V8. But as economies twitched, Porsche preferred to escape any 944 stigma, and move upwards. So in 1989 a successor for the 944 was given the nod, as Coupe and Cabriolet, as type number 968. Unlike the 944 it wouldn't be built by Audi but by Porsche themselves, it would be "80 per cent new" and it would be unveiled in summer 1991.

When the 968 appeared, the 944 heritage was clear to see, but the fixed-headlamp nose and broad tail were neater, stronger and more contemporary, with styling cues from the 928, the new Carreras, even the 959—confirming that this was more than ever a true Porsche and a serious performer.

The new shape might not have set any records for low drag, but it was more efficient as well as more striking, with Cd figures down to 0.34 for the Coupe and 0.35 for the low-roofed Cabriolet—which (particularly with the top up) was arguably the best looking of all 968s. It also claimed less high-speed tail lift, and it had more effective crash-protecting crumple zones. Emphasizing the "real Porsche" theme, it had new five-spoke alloy wheels similar to those on the new Turbo and Carrera RS, which not only looked good but also offered better brake cooling through their more open pattern.

The mechanical layout was also clearly 944, including the big four-cylinder engine with its thumping torque and smoothing counterbalance shafts, the highly effective transaxle and suspension layout (with revised settings), ABS brakes, power steering, and much of the 944's floorpan, center sections, roof and interior structure—all modified and updated, but all recognizably carry-overs. At launch, financial constraints meant there was no longer a Turbo, but the naturally-aspirated big-bore four followed the 3-liter, 16-valve basics of the 944 S2 engine, with some technically interesting and very effective updating. Most significant was VarioCam variable inlet-valve timing, allowing maximum low- and mid-range torque with optimum top-end power, complemented by improved manifolds, and lighter pistons and rods that allowed higher revs. Power and torque both jumped significantly, from 211 to 240bhp and 203 to 221lb. ft., while Porsche now offered the option of sending that through either a new six-speed manual gearbox or an improved, more "adaptive" four-speed Tiptronic.

A manual 968 coupe was good for 155mph and 0–60mph in 6.2 seconds but that was only the start. In 1993, Porsche followed the 911 RS philosophy with the 968 Club Sport—stripped and lightened in much the same way as its 911 cousin. With just two, race-style seats, lowered, widened, stiffened and with a bit more power, it became the quickest 968 for the least money—a car, again in the RS mould, for the uncompromising enthusiast. It was only the quickest, though, for a matter of months, until the inevitable Turbo version arrived. In this case, as the Turbo S, that was a strictly limited edition (running to just over 1900 cars) to qualify the 968 for the German GT championship. It was very powerful, with 305bhp, very quick, at over 175mph and with 0–60mph in 4.5 seconds, and very expensive. Or at the other end of the scale, for British customers only, there was the 968 Sport—a sort of mid-point between the cheap and driver-focused but very Spartan Club Sport and the mainstream 968 with its extensive list of creature comforts. That offered Club Sport reflexes and most of the performance with a few more luxuries, at a price considerably lower than the fully-equipped "comfort" models—and it sold well.

Or at least as well as the 968 was now able. Because inevitably, it couldn't go on forever. The basics were starting to show their age, build quality was slipping, and the market was changing. By mid-1995 the 968 was gone.

Left: The high tail of the 968 cabriolet is left bare, but the coupe has a small spoiler across the trailing edge of the window.

Below: Like its predecessor the 944, the "80 per cent new" 968 offered a handsome and versatile cabriolet version, which looked equally good with the double-lined and electrically operated hood either down or up.

Right The biggest changes between the looks of the 944 and those of the 968 are in the even smoother nose and tail treatments, which managed to give a family affinity with the 928 while still looking very individual.

Below Left: As well as looking good, the latest style of Porsche five-spoke alloy wheel—much as on the Turbo and RS 911s—offered more internal space for bigger brakes and more ventilation for better brake cooling.

Below Right: The body-colored door handles are a neat touch.

Below Left: The tail features single-color lenses fitting smoothly into the deformable plastic bumper, with internal filters to produce the appropriate light colors.

Below Right: The steeply-raked windscreen gives the car a look not unlike that of a classic mid-1950s Speedster.

SPECIFICATIONS

Engine Flat-six
Capacity 3600cc
Bore x stroke 100.0 x 76.4mm
Compression ratio 11.3:1
Power 272bhp
Valve gear Double overhead
  camshafts, four valves
  per cylinder
Fuel system Bosch Motronic
  engine management, fuel
  injection
Transmission Six-speed manual
Front suspension Independent,
  by MacPherson struts, coil
  springs, telescopic dampers,
  anti-roll bar
Rear suspension Independent,
  by double wishbones, coil
  springs, telescopic dampers,
  anti-roll bar
Brakes All ventilated discs
Wheels Bolt-on, light-alloy
Weight 3021lb. (1370kg)
Maximum speed 168mph
  (270kph)
Production 1993–97

911 Carrera (993)

By 1993, the essential 911 shape had acquired thirty years of familiarity factor since its original unveiling in Paris in 1963, and although an early 1990's 911 was very different in detail from an early 1960's one, there was absolutely no mistaking the heritage. Which was one of the reasons why many of the same people who worried about where 911 technology was going every time a new version came along were also very apprehensive when the new 993 generation promised a radically updated shape. But they needn't have been so concerned, because Porsche weren't about to break the mold completely.

They were about to make a major leap, though. Because beyond being just another 911 update, this was a genuinely new car—the biggest single departure from the evolutionary line so far in the 911's history, with a new platform, significantly different rear suspension layout, a heavily revised interior, improved clutch action and lighter gearshifts. A further revised 3.6-liter flat-six produced 272bhp in naturally aspirated form, or 360bhp in the latest version of the Turbo. Plus, of course, the new looks which more than anything underlined just how new the 993 generation was.

The new shape created arguably the best looking 911 of all, by achieving something that hardly seemed possible—making the 911's shape even simpler. Or at least smoother than ever, both visually and aerodynamically, with a new headlamp style and far better integrated front and rear bumper assemblies, which no longer appeared to be add-on components as they always had been. What's more, the new body was heavily updated under the skin, with new computer design processes making it usefully stiffer

but no heavier. And if anything, the smoother look made the latest 911 look even more toned, even more muscular but without being artificially pumped up with add-ons.

The interior changes were aimed at making the 911 more comfortable and more user-friendly, with much improved seats and a rather more effective new heater system. A new four-spoke steering wheel accommodated the now mandatory driver airbag—but there were still enough Porsche idiosyncrasies (especially the floor-mounted pedals) to mean it couldn't be anything but a 911.

Nor could the drivetrain, which was still one generation short of the impending switch from air- to water-cooling. So the essentials were entirely familiar, with the air-cooled flat-six behind the rear axle and a choice of either six-speed manual or four-speed Tiptronic automatic transaxles, the latter with a choice of fully automatic mode or one-touch clutchless manual shifts either through the central selector lever or steering-wheel buttons. But again, the details were extensively upgraded. Capacity carried over from the final 964 Carreras, at 3.6 liters, but plenty had changed inside. The crankshaft was strengthened and the pistons lightened to liberate more revs, more use was made of lightweight materials in the

Left: The 993 generation's updating of the classic 911 shape was in some ways the most radical so far, and the cause of some apprehension, but the faithful needn't have worried — the new car was in many ways the purest 911 shape yet.

Above Left: Neatness was almost an obsession with Porsche by this stage of the 911's evolution — even in something as basic as the graphics on the latest Tiptronic gearshift.

Above Right: However you looked at it, the 993 was still a 911.

ancillaries, and a new generation of Bosch electronic management was introduced—increasing peak output to 272bhp. One thing that did survive, however, was the snarling, woofling aural character—and that as much as anything was what confirmed that a 993 was still a 911.

Beyond the platform changes prompted by more modern design techniques and similarly improved production technologies, there was one fundamental chassis change. The familiar semi-trailing arm rear suspension became a multi-link layout, again with coil springs all round, but basically set up to be a little bit softer in standard form, with the option of a more extreme Sport pack comprising stiffer springs, dampers and anti-roll bars. And according to most testers, it was a successful program of revisions, because the new car was widely reckoned to have quicker and more communicative steering, better front to rear balance, and better front-end grip than the last 964s—which were generally thought to

have lost a bit of the earlier 911s' sharpness. Once again, Porsche had made a 911 that was more accessible to more ordinary drivers.

In another familiar progression, the brakes were even more powerful and responsive than ever, with ventilated and cross-drilled discs, four-piston calipers, and a new generation of ABS anti-lock as standard equipment.

All of which, naturally, became the foundation for another extended family of 911s, which kept on developing through the 993's relatively short production life of barely four years. There were Carrera 2s and 4s, a Cabriolet, a new kind of Targa, the Turbos (including the Turbo S) and the even more extreme versions such as the original GT2, and they were all outstanding. In fact by the time the water-cooled 996 family was due to replace the 993s in 1997, the general view was that the final 911s were the finest 911s of all. Now it was the next new generation that would have to persuade the cynics…

Right: Even with the more radical changes of the new generation, the key styling cues were still there if you knew where to look. Like the familiar fuel filler flap in the front wing, the distinctive rake of the headlamps, the neat air-intake recess in the top of the bonnet, and the unmistakable sweep of the side windows.

Above Left: The inside story was very much the same as the exterior – almost everything was new, but it all had a very familiar feel.

Above Right: Subtlety and quality had both made considerable strides – no more picnic tray wings now, and impeccable panel fits.

SPECIFICATIONS

Engine Flat-six
Capacity 3600cc
Bore x stroke 100.0 x 76.4mm
Compression ratio 11.3:1
Power 272bhp
Valve gear Double overhead
  camshafts, four valves
  per cylinder
Fuel system Bosch Motronic
  engine management, fuel
  injection
Transmission Six-speed manual
Front suspension Independent,
  by MacPherson struts, coil
  springs, telescopic dampers,
  anti-roll bar
Rear suspension Independent,
  by double wishbones, coil
  springs, telescopic dampers,
  anti-roll bar
Brakes All ventilated discs
Wheels Bolt-on, light-alloy
Weight 3021lb. (1370kg)
Maximum speed 168mph
  (270kph)
Production 1993–97

Carrera Cabriolet (993)

For production volume, coupes have represented the core of Porsche sales virtually from the start of production in 1950, with the original 356. But it's worth remembering that the very first design to wear the Porsche badge, the 356 Roadster of 1948, was actually an open car. And open models of various configurations have always been an important part of the range—even though the numbers built may have been in the minority. It's also true that the notion of a drop-top Porsche being nothing more complicated than a coupe with the roof chopped off is far from the truth. The open cars, from cabriolets and convertibles to roadsters, speedsters and targas, have always presented technical (and occasionally political) challenges of their own. Most important is that taking the top off a coupe is like taking the top off an egg, and it is very difficult to put all the necessary stiffness back into the car to maintain a solid platform and taut handling. Beyond that, it is more difficult to deliver consistent comfort, weather protection and refinement in an open-topped car. And not least, by the time the 911 came along, some markets were far more sensitive about roll-over protection issues, and passenger safety.

Still, a Cabriolet, bodied by specialist coachbuilder Beutler, was available in the 356 range from its first year of production. And for the 356, thanks largely to the encouragement of Max Hoffman and the American market, a Speedster followed the Cabriolet, and a Convertible and Roadster followed the Speedster, for both America and Europe, through the 1950s and into the 1960s. When the 911 family arrived, too, it was barely two years before it offered an open-top option. And that was another new layout, dubbed the Targa and named for Porsche's successes with its open sports racers in the classic Targa Florio road race. It was a new open-top

solution for a world of tougher regulations and increasing safety consciousness—especially in America, which by that time was by far Porsche's biggest market but which was threatening to make conventional convertibles, with their minimal rollover protection, a thing of the past. And the Targa, with its lift out roof panels and fixed roll hoop, proved a clever and popular solution to open-topped versatility with maximum safety.

As it transpired, however, the Targa was a solution to a problem that never actually arose, as America came to disapprove of traditional convertibles but never officially outlawed them. Also, as it turned out, it would be the only open 911 option for rather longer than might otherwise have been the case. So, remarkably, it was not until the early 1980s that Porsche introduced a full convertible model to the 911 range—in the form of the Carrera Cabriolet.

Having been shown as a "study" at the Geneva Show early in 1982, it was confirmed as a future production model alongside the latest 3-liter Carrera at the 1982 Frankfurt Show, some six months after the Geneva unveiling. And it was in production by the end of 1983, by which time Carrera power had grown to 3.2 liters and 231bhp—increasing again in 1988, to a full 250bhp. In 1987 the 964 generation Cabriolet was also offered for the first time with Turbo power, and by 1989 there was another variant—the re-emergence of the Speedster philosophy, with low windscreen and a more simply engineered low canvas roof which retracted under a bulky rigid cover behind the cockpit. It was supposedly shaped to improve the aerodynamics, but was not exactly pretty.

That would be the last 911 from Zuffenhausen to use a derivative of the original body shape, and it survived to the end of the 964 line. But when the 911 reached its ultimate air-cooled incarnation in the totally re-shaped and

Right: Although coupes have nearly always represented the core of Porsche sales, the very first was an open car—the 356 Roadster of 1948. Open models have always been an important part of the range, and have always presented technical challenges of their own since—without the stiffness provided by the roof—it is hard to maintain a solid platform and taut handling.

Above: The simply-engineered low canvas roof retracted under a bulky rigid cover behind the cockpit. It was supposedly shaped to improve the aerodynamics, but was not exactly pretty.

ultra-sleek 993 range, from 1993, although the Speedster was finally dropped, the Cabriolet again became a core part of the family (in two- or four-wheel drive 272bhp Carrera versions). And soon afterwards, Porsche also added a completely new spin on the Targa. A brilliantly effective and very handsome spin, too, which was much closer to the standard coupe shape than any previous Targa had been. It featured an all-glass central roof section, in thermally-filtered glass, which was electrically retractable at

the touch of a button, between strong side rails that were a lot neater than the old Targa's rear roll-hoop.

Like the latest Cabriolet, it featured the new 285bhp 3.6 flat-six, and either six-speed manual or four-speed Tiptronic S automatic transmissions. And while the Targa was fractionally heavier than the Coupe, the new Cabriolet was actually lighter, accelerated faster and gave away almost nothing on maximum speed. As Autocar said, "a no-compromise supercar, even with no roof."

Left: Although it was more difficult to to deliver consistent weather protection in an open-topped car, the Carrera Cabriolet interior certainly did not compromise on comfort and refinement.

Right: Compared with the Coupe, the new Cabriolet was lighter, accelerated faster and gave away almost nothing on maximum speed.

Right: Although tougher regulations and a new safety-consciousness had threatened the existence of open-top cars, even America had failed to ban them completely.

Below: A no-compromise supercar—even with no roof.

Boxster/Boxster S

It was a long-running dilemma: with the demise of the 968, Porsche lost yet another sub-911 "volume" car, but still needed to fill that commercially vital gap. Enter the Boxster. Alongside the new 911, another Porsche, to give two distinct lines—different in looks, layout, price range and target market, to exploit new production efficiencies and appeal to a broader market. And thanks to parallel development, a second range for a relatively bearable investment.

It debuted in Detroit in January 1993, as the Boxster concept. The rave reviews were undoubtedly welcome, as Porsche had given a production version of the Boxster the go-ahead almost a year earlier, to sell eventually alongside the equally new 911. Less than three years later, the Boxster was signed off—which seemed a long wait to some, but given the scale and complexity of developing two designs at once was actually quite an achievement. Because, for both cars, this was as close as Porsche come to starting with a clean-sheet.

Some moaned, too, that the production Boxster lost the concept's purity, but in adapting to stringent legal requirements (especially in meeting crash-test rules), it actually changed surprisingly little. Dimensions and details evolved subtly, but only to make it street-legal and buildable—and if the concept's wild cockpit design was diluted, at least it became practicable, and while it was rather simpler than a 911's, it was clearly related. From nose to screen, it was almost identical to the forthcoming 911. Behind that, the Boxster had an edge, in offering either lift-off hardtop or power soft-top. Further back still, it was different again—genuinely mid-, not rear-engined. And if that made it purely a two-seater, it was a very practical one, with impressive luggage space in both front and rear boots. It also gave the Boxster a character of its own.

It previewed the all-new water-cooled flat-six destined for the new 911, albeit in smaller, mechanically simpler and slightly milder guise. It had four cams, four valves per cylinder, variable inlet-valve timing and dry-sump lubrication. As launched, its 2.5 liters (compared to the 911's 3.4) delivered 204bhp, through either five-speed manual or five-speed Tiptronic S transmissions—the latter with steering-wheel-mounted thumb shifts for the sequential clutchless manual mode. There was power steering and all-disc brakes backed by ABS, while suspension used struts and lower arms at the front, struts and multiple links behind, all with coil springs, gas dampers, anti-roll bars, and lots of light alloy components.

So if it was less potent than a 911, in other ways the Boxster was as brilliant as any Porsche to date. 150mph-plus and 0–60mph in 6.9 seconds for the manual version were

fine for most users, but the real joy was in the superb balance of ride and handling, and the Boxster's youthfully sporty personality.

Build quality shone through in everything from fit and finish to the shell's obvious stiffness on poor surfaces, and that stiffness was also the foundation for brilliant body control and impeccable feel. With almost perfect front-to-rear balance it was notably less tail-happy than a 911, and less sensitive to cross winds at speed, but it also had levels of agility and precision in the finest Porsche traditions. Crucially, too, while feeling similar enough to a 911 to be part of the family, it was different enough to create a following of its own.

And it did, in spades. Launched for 1997 it broke away from the image of a "poor man's" Porsche and simply became an alternative Porsche, all-new but brimming with the classic genes. It was so good out of

the box, in fact, that it has simply evolved rather than changed dramatically. Basically, Porsche has progressively given the Boxster more of a performance "edge." The early sport package added retuned suspension and bigger wheels, then in 1999 2.7 liters and 220bhp (and later 228) pushed performance ahead slightly, and flexibility enormously. And alongside that in 1999 came the next big leap, in the Boxster S.

Pending the promised arrival of a 320bhp Boxster Turbo for mid-2005, this was the one for anyone who still thought a Boxster wasn't quite potent enough to be a real 911 alternative. Except for a neat additional front-dam airscoop, twin tail-pipes and red brake calipers gripping bigger discs, it didn't look very different. But it was, with 3.2 liters/246bhp, making even better use of those sublime chassis dynamics. By 2002 it could boast 260bhp, and mild styling revisions inside and out. It just kept getting better.

Below: The Boxster was meant to signal a fresh start, the best possible "entry-level" Porsche for a new century. Demand was such that Porsche had to buy in additional assembly capacity from a specialist in Finland, and for the 2000 model year they introduced the 3.2-liter, 252bhp Boxster S.

Right: Although recognizably still shaped by the same experienced team, the compact, affordable Boxster reversed the old tendency to spread, to put on weight, and to put on cost.

Above: The concept car's wild cockpit design was diluted and became more practicable, and although it was simpler than a 911's, it was obviously related. There were also fully-trimmed luggage compartments at front and rear.

Above: The Boxster offered either a lift-off hardtop or a power soft-top, and a rear spoiler rose up to do its stabilizing duty at speeds of 50mph and more.

Above: The first truly modern, well-laid out and user-friendly fascia/instrument display for more than two decades. Mutterings about the need for more performance and equipment were settled in future years as the options list built up.

Left: As an open-top two-seater—a real sports car, as opposed to a large coupe with the top cropped off—in many ways the Boxster was a throwback to the much-loved Speedster of the 1950s.

SPECIFICATIONS

Engine Flat-six, water-cooled
Capacity 3200cc
Bore x stroke 95.0 x 74.4mm
Compression ratio 9.3:1
Power 544bhp (road version)
Valve gear Four overhead
   camshafts, four valves
   per cylinder
Fuel system
Transmission Six-speed manual
Front suspension Double
   wishbones, coil springs,
   telescopic dampers,
   anti-roll bar
Rear suspension Double
   wishbones, coil springs,
   telescopic dampers,
   anti-roll bar
Brakes All discs, ventilated and
   cross-drilled
Wheels Multi-spoke light alloy
   racing type, center-lock
Weight 2755lb. (250kg)
Maximum speed 192mph
   (307kph–limited for road)
Production From 1996 to
   1998, road versions
   produced to homologate
   racing version, and had to
   be sold for "less than
   $1,000,000"

GTI

The ultimate first generation 911 road car was also the ultimate expression of racing needs creating extreme cars—and they didn't come any more extreme than the 911 GT1. It was created for the most exotic end of the Le Mans rule book of the late 1990s, and designed to be an outright Le Mans winner. As such, it was designed to a familiar theme, obliging Porsche to build (and sell) a large enough number of customer cars to satisfy the homologation requirements. And because the rules also required it, beyond the customer racing versions there had to be a road-legal version, and under this particular generation of rules that had to sell for less than $1,000,000. So not exactly an everyday Porsche, but at least another one that had to have a genuine roadgoing connection.

Astonishingly, it was again rooted in the apparently indestructible 911. In fact, more than that, it bridged a forthcoming gap, between the first and second generations of Porsche's icon. It was unveiled in 1996, and the starting point really was a virtually standard 911 front chassis section. Around that, Porsche grafted a carbonfiber and Kevlar composite tub and bodywork, on a stretched wheelbase, with long nose and tail for optimum high-speed dynamics, no rear window, and an air intake mounted on the leading edge of the roof, cutting slightly into the top edge of the low, steeply raked windscreen.

The intake feeds a very spectacular engine, even by Porsche standards. Previewing the next generation of more

conventional 911s, the 3.2-liter flat-six is water-cooled, with four cams, and four valves per cylinder. It sat where the rear seats would have been in any lesser 911, ahead of the gearbox for a true mid-engined layout. It had extremely exotic internals, of course, and twin turbochargers—which delivered a staggering 544bhp even in the road car. Oddly, perhaps, but probably quite sensibly, in road trim it was electronically limited to a maximum of 192mph, but it would reach 60mph from rest in not much more than 3.5 seconds. And of course it was rear-drive only.

Inside, amazingly, it looked even more like a regular 911 than it did outside, and in road trim was actually very well trimmed and quite comfortable. Naturally, the cabin was protected by a complex and hefty roll cage structure, but it also had leather coverings for the high-backed, wing-sided bucket seats (borrowed from the Carrera RS), and it had a more or less standard 911 dashboard layout. On the other hand, it did have bare carbonfiber door-liner panels, and an exposed gear-selector linkage running through the cockpit from the high-mounted lever to the windowless bulkhead behind the seats.

It crammed all kinds of cooling intake and exit vents into the wide front and rear wings, in the nose and where the rear quarter-windows would normally be, and it had a massive, high-mounted rear wing as well as the tall airdam on top of the tail, and extensive underbody aerodynamic trickery. And under that not particularly pretty but

extremely effective shape (which could provide positive downforce at high speeds, even in road trim) it had much the same pure racing suspension layout as the 956 and 963 prototype racers of a few years before. Plus astoundingly powerful brakes with near 15-inch diameter ventilated and cross-drilled discs grabbed by eight-piston calipers—and all squeezed inside huge 18-inch diameter center-lock multi-spoke wheels.

It served its purpose in every significant respect. Even at only a few Deutschmarks short of the mandatory million-dollar ceiling, it found customers, and it found other customers in pure racing form, too. But the ultimate success for the ultimate 911 came from the works cars, at Le Mans. Ironically, on its first appearance in the 24-hour classic, in 1996, the two works 911 GT1s were beaten into second and third places by the older TWR-built Spyder run by the Joest team in the prototype category. In 1997 the first evolution GT1s lost the lead with mechanical problems near the end of the race, leaving Joest to win again. But in 1998, with all new bodywork and a carbonfiber chassis, they made it third time lucky, with a hard-fought one-two victory, led by the driver teaming of Allan McNish, Stéphane Ortelli and Laurent Aiello—in Porsche's fiftieth anniversary year. And although it was hugely successful in other major races, for Le Mans, that was the GT1's swansong, before the rules changed again. But as a racer with a tax disc, the GT1 had made its point long before that.

Top: The ultimate success for the ultimate 911 came from the works cars, at Le Mans, but even at only a few Deutschmarks short of the mandatory million-dollar ceiling, it found customers, both on the road and in pure racing form.

Above: The water-cooled 3.2-liter flat-six sat where the rear seats would have been in a lesser 911, ahead of the gearbox for a true mid-engined layout. The twin turbochargers delivered a staggering 544bhp even in the road car. In road trim it was electronically limited to a maximum of 192mph, but it would reach 60mph from rest in not much more than 3.5 seconds.

Left: Designed to be an outright Le Mans winner, the GT1 was the most extreme street-legal Porsche. Despite its exotic background it was based on the 911—and it came to bridge the gap between the first and second generations of the Porsche icon.

SPECIFICATIONS

Engine Flat-six
Capacity 3387cc
Bore x stroke 96.0 x 78.0mm
Compression ratio 10.4:1
Power 296bhp
Valve gear Double overhead camshafts, four valves per cylinder
Fuel system Bosch Motronic engine management, fuel injection
Transmission Six-speed manual
Front suspension Independent, by MacPherson struts, coil springs, telescopic dampers, anti-roll bar
Rear suspension Independent, by multi-links, coil springs, telescopic dampers, anti-roll bar
Brakes All ventilated discs
Wheels Bolt-on, light-alloy
Weight 2911lb. (1320kg)
Maximum speed 173mph (278kph)
Production 1997–to date

911 Coupe (996)

This was the biggest leap in 911 development for more than thirty years, since the original 911 replaced the 356. It was officially Type 996, but according to the badges it was still a 911, and by most other criteria it was a 911, too.

It was new from the ground up, and had to be, because things had moved on a long way since the first 911 appeared—in terms of legislation, customer expectations, even in how Porsche had evolved into a much more sophisticated company. So such a car would have to be safer, cleaner, more practical, more economical, but just as quick and characterful. Yet Porsche's core market still wanted the 911, so Porsche built one for a new generation.

It was quite different from the original in shape, size, and even proportions. It was bigger, to satisfy new crash-test requirements, new demands for space and practicality, and not least to include radiators for a water-cooled engine. But the cues that remained were so strong that it clearly was a 911. If some reckoned it had lost a bit of character, or muscle tone, they could hardly argue that it didn't fit the Porsche mold of stylish functionality. It was different inside, too, with a radically more modern dashboard and control details, new pedal layout and improved driving position, a bit more space and perceived quality—but again with enough classic 911 cues to evoke the original.

Further advantages of the all-new shell meant the new 911 could be stronger and safer but lighter, easier to build and easier to repair; and it was now genuinely as aerodynamic as it had always looked—bringing the Cd figure down from 0.34 to 0.30, while reducing high-speed lift.

The biggest change, though, was to water-cooling, because refinement, compact packaging and meeting stringent noise and emissions rules were now more important than saving weight, complexity and

manufacturing costs—which had been the needs behind Dr Porsche's original air-cooled engine design, for his "people's car." Not that this was Porsche's first venture into water-cooling with the flat engines. The 959, and various racing models, had used water-cooled heads, and most recently both the GT1 racer and the new Boxster had been completely water-cooled, as was the new 996. So the new all-alloy flat-six arrived with a capacity of 3.4 liters, forged seven-bearing crankshaft, forged pistons, dry-sump lubrication, and radiators in the front of the car—two on six-speed manual models, three on the five-speed button-shift Tiptronic S automatic ones, including a third radiator for the transmission fluid. It had four camshafts, four valves per cylinder, Variocam variable inlet timing, variable volume intakes and state-of-the-art electronic management. The electronics also introduced Automatic Brake Differential, piggy-backing the ABS system to deter wheelspin on slippery surfaces. And although capacity was smaller than its air-cooled Carrera predecessor, efficiency had improved to the extent that it was more powerful (as well as cleaner and more fuel efficient), with a peak of 300bhp.

The stiffer shell carried re-designed coil-spring suspension (incorporating numerous aluminum components). It had totally revised steering, and race-bred brakes with light-alloy four-piston calipers grabbing huge ventilated and cross-drilled discs—inside larger diameter alloy wheels, with even bigger "sport-pack" options. With the longer wheelbase and wider tracks it offered comfort as well as control, and naturally there were those who equated that to the 911 losing its edge. The truth, though, was that the 911 had become more modern, and in some ways more

Above: The all-new shell meant the new 911 could be stronger and safer but lighter, easier to build and easier to repair; and it was now genuinely as aerodynamic as it had always looked—bringing the Cd figure down from 0.34 to 0.30, while reducing high-speed lift.

Below: The new 911 coupe was quite different from the original in shape, size, and even proportions. It was bigger, to satisfy new crash-test requirements, new demands for space and practicality—and not least to include radiators for a water-cooled engine. But despite all this, it clearly was a 911.

conventional, because it had to, while abandoning its roots far less dramatically than the skeptics wanted to believe.

It was less demanding to drive, a bit quieter and more compliant, with generally lighter controls and less hair-trigger character, but in everyday driving for everyday drivers, it was a better car for it. It was still quick, with a top speed nudging 175mph, 0–60mph in less than five seconds and 100mph in under eleven. And it still had an almost unrivalled blend of grip and control, but with added civility and long-distance refinement. It retained the

underlying characteristics of the rear-engined layout, even the ultimate flaws of any other 911, but now with a much more forgiving nature. In short, the outer limits of its roadholding were now more accessible for more drivers, which was precisely what Porsche had set out to achieve. So while there was no denying that the last of the previous generation 911s was more focused and more rawly exciting in the right hands, on the right roads, and in smallish doses, it was just as true that the new one was exactly what a 911 now had to be.

Above: Safety legislation had changed very dramatically in the years between the appearance of the first generation 911 and the 996 generation. The 996 shows off its impact-absorbing structures.

Right: With its longer wheelbase, the 911 offered comfort as well as control—and naturally there were those who equated that to it losing its edge. However, although it had become more modern—and perhaps more conventional—it had certainly not abandoned its roots.

Above: the spacious cab included a wide variety of electronic equipment—a far cry from the earliest Porsches with their simple instrument panels.

Above: Stopping has always been as important to Porsche as going, and the braking specification of the 996 was typically heavy duty, with massive ventilated and cross-drilled discs all round.

SPECIFICATIONS

Engine Flat-six, water-cooled
Capacity 3600cc
Bore x stroke 96.0 x 82.8mm
Compression ratio 11.3:1
Power 320bhp
Valve gear Four overhead camshafts, four valves per cylinder, variable valve timing
Fuel system Fuel injected
Transmission Six-speed manual, or five-speed Tiptronic, four-wheel drive
Front suspension MacPherson strut with lateral and longitudinal control links, conical coil springs and telescopic dampers
Rear suspension Multi-link, with coil springs and telescopic dampers
Brakes All disks, ABS
Wheels Alloy, Turbo-style
Weight 3295lb. (1495kg)
Maximum speed 175mph (280kph)
Production 996 generation Carrera 4S introduced 2001

911 Carrera 4S

From the day the original 911 Turbo was launched, creating impressive new levels of performance and a very different dynamic personality from its non-turbo siblings, the debate has raged: Turbo power or unadulterated Carrera responses? Outright performance or sheer, uncomplicated character? Aggressive Turbo looks or Carrera understatement? Not to mention Turbo prices and insurance premiums versus Carrera ones. And of course, with the 996-family 911, none of that changed, as the new Carrera 4S proved beyond doubt.

Launched in 2001, the first 996-type Carrera 4S wasn't the first Carrera 4S of all—that had appeared as a late addition to the 993 generation, for the 1994 model year. It had set the pattern for those who were happy with the power of a Carrera but preferred the visual presence of a Turbo. In a nutshell, the latest generation Carrera 4S, just like its predecessor, is what happens when you cross the best bits of the Turbo's chassis and aerodynamic packaging, plus its four-wheel drive

transmission layout, with the naturally-aspirated flat-six which powers the majority of the range—then stir in some unique details and fine tuning of the car's own. And to some people that marriage created arguably the best all-rounder in the mainstream heart of the "new 911" line-up.

Visually, the Carrera 4S is more Turbo than Carrera, with its mixture of wide wheel arches, more conspicuous air intakes and exits and more aggressive aerodynamics. But under the skin it delivers an intriguing crossover of technologies. For one thing, it acknowledges that absolute power isn't everything, and even admits that, in some respects, power can indeed corrupt. And for another it accepts that while four-wheel drive undoubtedly does compromise ultimate feel, the benefits in security are worth the penalty.

Above: At the rear of the 911 Carrera 4S there is an automatic spoiler. The red light strip forms a visual link between the rear lights.

So the heart of the Turbo-lookalike Carrera 4S is the latest version of the 996 family's water-cooled flat-six, whose capacity had been increased for Carrera models in 2001, from the original 3.4 liters to 3.6 liters. That in turn pushed maximum power up from 300bhp to 320bhp, and further improved the already impressive torque spread—which now peaked with 273lb. ft. and helped the Carrera 4S to 60mph from a standstill in exactly five seconds, on its way to a maximum speed of more than 175mph. And although that meant the 4S gave away exactly 100bhp to the current Turbo, there were plenty of 911 lovers who were happy to trade an extra 15mph or so, and maybe a second off the 0–60mph time, for the razor sharp throttle responses and generally more linear performance characteristics of the naturally-aspirated car over the turbocharged one—especially when the other advantage was a more than token price saving.

Above: Although the 4S gave away exactly 100bhp to the Turbo, it could still do 0–60mph from standstill in five seconds and had a maximum speed of more than 175mph.

Left: Fitted across the 911 range, the VarioCam Plus system combines variable valves on the intake camshaft with a switchable valve lift system, allowing both the opening and closing times of the intake valves to be varied, as well as the amount of valve lift used.

Left: The 911 Carrera 4S adopted the wide-bodied looks of the 911 Turbo, with wide wheel arches, conspicuous air intakes and exits, and aggressive aerodynamics. However, under the skin it acknowledges that absolute power isn't everything.

SPECIFICATIONS

Engine Flat-six
Capacity 3600cc
Bore x stroke 100.0 x 76.4mm
Compression ratio 9.4:1
Power 420bhp
Valve gear Double overhead camshafts, four valves per cylinder
Fuel system Bosch DME engine management, fuel injection, twin turbochargers
Transmission Six-speed manual (Tiptronic five-speed automatic with permanent four-wheel-drive optional)
Front suspension Independent, by double wishbones, coil springs, telescopic dampers, anti-roll bar
Rear suspension Independent, by double wishbones, coil springs, telescopic dampers, anti-roll bar
Brakes All ventilated discs
Wheels Bolt-on, light-alloy
Weight 3396lb. (1540kg)
Maximum speed 189mph (305kph)
Production 1999–to date

911 Turbo (996)

Above: The 911 Turbo commands a top speed of 190mph (3056km/h) and accelerates from 0–60mph (0–100km/h) in a mere 4.2 seconds.

Below: When it was launched, in 1974, its giant leap in power and performance made the Turbo arguably Porsche's first supercar. The latest Turbo follows the heritage.

In the 1970s, the birth of the first generation 911 Turbo was Porsche's way of standing the supercar establishment on its head. In one mighty blow (literally) the Turbo snatched back the initiative from arch rivals Ferrari and Lamborghini by proving that there was more to ultimate performance than a dozen cylinders under the bonnet and a designer nameplate on the body shell. When it was launched, in 1974, its giant leap in power and performance made the Turbo arguably Porsche's first true supercar, as opposed to very fast sports car. And it defined the levels of performance Porsche enthusiasts would henceforth take for granted at the sharp end of the Porsche range. So it was no surprise that the Turbo was here to stay, and that even when the 911 moved into a new generation, the Turbo would still be a major part of the recipe.

The original car, remember, had been created as much to further Porsche's interests on the racetrack as in the showroom, and at a time when turbocharging was already a powerful force in motor sport (not least in Porsche's own 1000bhp CanAm racers) but still a rarity on production cars. More than just satisfying racing homologation rules while re-defining peak Porsche roadcar performance though, it proved the existence of a market for supercar performance combined with a degree of luxury. And selling at a price far higher than anything else in the range, it proved there was profit in the formula, too.

Starting with 3.0 liters and 260bhp it grew through 3.3 liters and 300bhp by 1978, to 330bhp for 1986, and by the time the air-cooled 911 generation reached its zenith, the Turbo boasted 408bhp and the limited edition Turbo S sported no less than 450bhp, for maxima beyond 180mph and 0–60mph times of less than four seconds—and still with the same up-market packaging.

That, perhaps, was why the skeptics couldn't accept that the new water-cooled 911, with or without a turbocharger, could ever match the focus of the air-cooled original—but when the first of the water-cooled Turbos joined the range in 2000, they mostly had to admit that it was still pretty special.

With twin turbochargers, the new 3.6-liter water-cooled flat-six delivered 420bhp, making it the most powerful mainstream Turbo so far—and the fastest. With two smaller, fast-reacting turbochargers instead of the earlier, big single unit, it also added new levels of low- and mid-range response to the already impressive mid- and top-end power, further redefining the Turbo's real world drivability—in what by supercar standards is still a compact and practical car. And, by any standards, it had astounding performance, headlined by a maximum of around 190mph, 0–60mph in less than four seconds, and 0–100mph in less than ten, with astonishing mid-range flexibility and responses. Just like the normally aspirated new-generation, too, it was big on refinement and civility.

Above: The new 3.6-liter, water-cooled, flat-six engine delivered 420bhp, making it the most powerful mainstream Turbo so far—and the fastest. The two smaller, fast-reacting turbochargers instead of the earlier big single unit also added new levels of low- and mid-range response to impressive mid- and top-end power.

Other things, too, had moved on some way from the relative simplicity of the original mid-1970s Turbo. Citing its massive torque, that car made do with a four-speed manual gearbox, but the new generation, with even more torque, offered a six-speed manual or the option of a fingertip-controlled five-speed Tiptronic automatic transmission. And where the original was rear-drive only, the 2000 Turbo had the sophistication of four-wheel drive, with a clever torque distribution system to get power instantly to where it could best be used. To ensure that it still behaved like a 911, though, the bias was always to the rear.

Suspension was essentially the same as on the naturally aspirated Carrera, but lowered and stiffened, and sitting on 18-inch alloy wheels with hollow spokes as part of a tire-pressure-sensing system which could alert the driver to possible loss of tire pressure before it became a major problem. And in classic Porsche tradition, braking power was more than equal to performance, thanks to

huge ventilated and cross-drilled disc brakes and four-piston calipers, derived in this case from the race-bred GT3. That was backed by Porsche's most advanced ABS system to date, which also formed the basis of the PSM Porsche Stability Management package, which used a combination of electronic throttle override and selective brake applications to control incipient loss of grip.

Otherwise, the new Turbo followed the subtler, more sophisticated character of the new "996" generation to a tee. The interior was just as stylish and luxurious, build and material quality just as conspicuous, practicality just as impressive, and packaging just as understated. In fact the visible differences between new Carrera and new Turbo were noticeably less extreme than between original Carrera and original Turbo—but the performance gains were every bit as impressive, whichever the generation.

Left: The original car had been created as much to further Porsche's interests on the racetrack as in the showroom. At the time, turbocharging was a powerful force in motor sport, but was still a rarity on production cars. Now turbocharging was commonplace, but the 911 Turbo certainly wasn't.

SPECIFICATIONS

Engine Flat-six, water-cooled
Capacity 3600cc
Bore x stroke 100.0 x 76.4mm
Compression ratio 11.7:1
Power 381bhp
Valve gear Four overhead
  camshafts, four valves per
  cylinder, variable valve timing
Fuel system Sequential
  multi-point fuel injection,
  electronic throttle
Transmission Six-speed manual
Front suspension MacPherson
  struts, coil springs, telescopic
  dampers, anti-roll bar
Rear suspension Multi-link, coil
  springs, telescopic dampers,
  anti-roll bar
Brakes All discs, ceramic discs
  optional
Wheels Light alloy
Weight 3035lb. (1377kg)
Maximum speed 191mph
  (306kph)
Production Latest version
  introduced 2003

911 GT2/GT3

When the water-cooled "new generation" 911 was launched in 1997, there were almost as many skeptics as there had been for the first 911, 34 years earlier. It couldn't be a 911 without air-cooling, or a proper 911 if it was too comfortable or well equipped, too smooth or respectable. Wrong. Old-school 911 lovers may have feared the new-school "996" was the beginning of the end for their beloved icon, but it was a new beginning. They should have known that if the first of the new 911s didn't match the outer-limits performance of the fastest of the old generation, it wouldn't be long before Porsche created one that would.

At Porsche, everything changes except the philosophy: Porsche make real sports cars. So on one level the new water-cooled 911 was soon followed up by the new generation water-cooled 911 Turbo. With 420bhp, a six-speed gearbox (or adaptive five-speed one-touch Tiptronic auto), four-wheel drive, electronic stability control, and the luxury and comfort of air-conditioning and leather trim, that was a 911 for those who prefer civilized manners and a touch of comfort beyond the 190mph top speed and 0–60mph acceleration in around 4.2 seconds. On the other hand, for those who like their performance with a slightly rawer edge, Porsche revived another 911 tradition which had started in the 1970s with the stripped to the bone RS and later the 911 Club Sport. For them, there would be the GT3—following the less-is-more philosophy.

The GT3 is the new 911 without frills, created purely for performance with creature comforts a very minor consideration. And as its name suggests, like many Porsches before it, the hidden agenda was motor sport—in this case to build enough customer cars to qualify this new generation 911 for the GT3 "production" racing category, where Porsche remained the make to beat.

To reach the homologation requirement, Porsche created a 911 GT3 road car that became one of the fastest in the world. All the old cues are there. It sits lower, wider, more aggressively muscled than the super-smooth mainstream model, with deep sill extensions, ground-hugging front and rear airdams, and a huge two-tier rear wing that's a worthy modern spin on the old 911 picnic tray. There are glimpses through the spidery, multi-spoke, split-rim 18-inch alloy wheels of race-bred, red-painted, four-piston alloy brake calipers and huge 13-inch ventilated and cross-drilled discs, while the suspension has been retuned around stiffer springs and dampers, even adjustable anti-roll bars.

The GT3 has ABS, which was unusual for a car with a racing role, but no feedback-dulling four-wheel drive (which wasn't permissible under GT3 rules), no restricting traction or stability controls—only uncorrupted responses to driver input. And it has performance. In road guise it isn't as stripped out as its RS and Club Sport predecessors (it even has air-conditioning and electric windows) but it does have racing-style, fixed-back bucket seats and an air of functionality.

It is powered by a naturally aspirated 3.6-liter version of the 911's all-alloy, four-cam, 24-valve flat-six, producing 360bhp, but more importantly instantaneous throttle responses and

a broad spread of usable power—which translates into highly adjustable handling in the hands of a skilled driver. A roadgoing GT3 will nudge 190mph and reach 60mph in less than 4.5 seconds, and in that respect isn't much different from a 911 Turbo, but in all other respects—especially ride and handling balance and feedback, the two could hardly be more different.

The downside to the GT3 is that it was a rare Porsche indeed. Having built enough cars to satisfy its primary purpose of racing homologation, in 1999 Porsche stopped building it. But the one thing we should know by now about extreme Porsches is there'll always be another one along soon. And so it was with the new 911 family, as Porsche followed the GT3 with the even more extreme GT2—an all-new successor to the 911 GT2s that had raced through the late 1990s. Like the GT3 it boasted 3.6 liters, but this one was turbocharged, with a massive 455bhp, yet it still fed it all through the rear wheels only, for an even more extreme version of the GT3's race-focused purity. It was even more muscular, with wide body and aggressive aerodynamic add-ons—it even had a roll-cage on the options list. It was staggeringly quick, obviously, with a top speed close to 200mph and 0–60mph in a blink over four seconds. While it didn't have quite the purity and communication of the GT3, (959 and GT1 apart) it was another fastest-ever 911. And, of course, another 911 icon.

Above: One of the fastest road cars in the world. It sits lower, and is wider and more aggressively muscled than the mainstream model.

Above: The 911 GT3 was created as a performance car, with creature comforts a very minor consideration.

Above and Below: The styling of the GT3 included deep sill extensions, ground-hugging front and rear airdams, and a huge, two-tier rear wing that is a worthy modern spin on the old 911 picnic table. The hidden agenda was motor sport—Porsche needed to build enough customer cars to qualify for the GT3 "production" racing category.

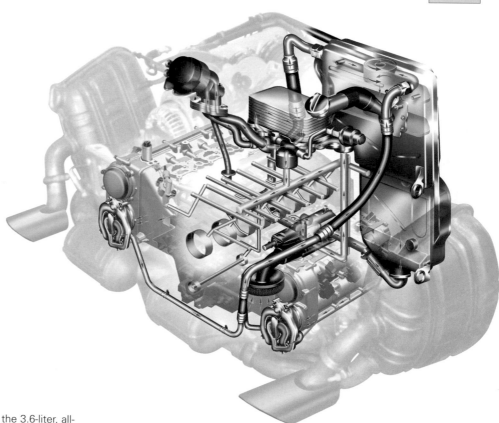

Above Right: The oil circuit of the 3.6-liter, all-alloy, four-cam 24-valve flat-six engine.

Right: The interior is not as stripped out as its RS and Club Sport predecessors, but it does have racing-style, fixed-back bucket seats.

Below Right: The huge, 13-inch, ventilated and cross-drilled Porsche ceramic composite brake.

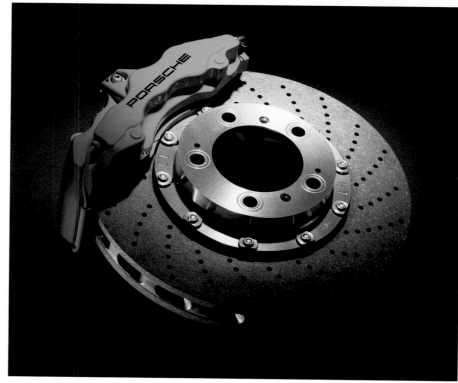

SPECIFICATIONS

Engine V8, water-cooled, twin turbochargers

Capacity 4500cc

Bore x stroke 93.0 x 83.0mm

Compression ratio 9.5:1

Power 450bhp

Valve gear Four overhead camshafts, four valves per cylinder, variable valve timing

Fuel system Fuel injected

Transmission Six-speed Tiptronic, four-wheel drive

Front suspension Double-track control arm axle, multi-mode air springs

Rear suspension Multi-link, multi-mode air springs

Brakes All ventilated discs, ABS

Wheels Alloy

Weight 5190lb. (2355kg)

Maximum speed 165mph (264kph)

Production Introduced 2002

Cayenne

Through their history, with virtually every new design, Porsche have courted controversy, but no new Porsche stirred as many feelings as the coming of the Cayenne—a very different kind of Porsche indeed. Launched in 2002, the Cayenne took the debate about what makes a Porsche a Porsche way beyond the usual realms of where the engine was located and how it was cooled, even about which wheels were driven and how it looked. The Cayenne is an SUV.

That's Sports Utility Vehicle—or put another way, a 4x4, a Porsche off-roader. But if it seemed that Porsche had finally turned their back on the old adage "cobbler stick to your last," it wasn't that cut and dried. Because when it finally appeared, the Cayenne also turned out to be a very sporty SUV indeed.

It brought a third line back to the Porsche range, and that more than anything explained why it was created: Porsche still needed to expand into new and lucrative areas, and one of the strongest was for up-market Sports Utilities with the emphasis on roadgoing performance. In the end, it was more a case of them no longer being able to avoid the sector than having to force themselves to join it. So the Cayenne was conceived as Porsche's "cross-country car."

It would have to compete with luxury rivals like the BMW X5, Mercedes M Class, the Lexus RX and the king of them all, the new and brilliant Range Rover—each of which offered decent performance and car-like on-road dynamics with varying levels of off-road ability (in the case of the Range Rover huge ability). So while Porsche were used to building "lifestyle" cars, this one would aspire to a lifestyle that Porsche hadn't embraced before. In fact to be truly successful it would have to make a crossover beyond the usual one between on-road and off-road abilities. It would have to convince SUV enthusiasts that Porsche could make an SUV that worked, and it would have to convince Porsche enthusiasts that an SUV could genuinely wear a Porsche badge. A tough call, but when the car finally reached production, it seemed Porsche had done it.

Autocar magazine welcomed it as "the off-roader that thinks it's a 911," or "Porsche's 4x4 supercar," and that would have been music to Porsche's ears. Ever since spy pictures of the Cayenne had started to appear, they had listened to criticisms that it looked bland (or worse) as well as the ongoing moans that a 4x4 simply couldn't be a real Porsche. But consider the specification of the Cayenne Turbo that took the car into production late in 2002.

It's a big package, with four doors and five seats—another Porsche first. Inside, it is roomy, comfortable and comprehensively equipped. It is more luxurious than functional, and while it looks very different from any other Porsche, it is far more Sport than Utility. It is powered by a compact, all-new, all-alloy 4.5-liter four-cam, four-valve V8 with VarioCam timing. In Turbo form that has a huge 450bhp and 457lb. ft. of torque, which makes the Cayenne Turbo comfortably the fastest off-roader in the world, with a maximum of 165mph and 0–62mph in 5.6 seconds—figures many sports cars would love to match.

Even the lower-priced alternative, the naturally-aspirated Cayenne S, has a more than useful 335bhp. It has all-independent air-spring suspension with wishbones at the front and multiple links at the rear. It has assisted rack and pinion steering, huge ventilated disc brakes, six-speed automatic transmission and a highly sophisticated electronically-controlled four-wheel drive system—with a rear-biased basic torque split because Porsche aren't afraid to let it oversteer. And it has Porsche's PSM stability control system, but the natural handling, body control and stability are so good that that is rarely needed.

Its on-road handling is better than any other luxury, sporting 4x4's—even the ones that emphasize on-road ability first and foremost. Yet off-road, the Cayenne also proved capable way beyond pre-launch expectations (though, of course, not Porsche's own). Even on rubber rated for over 185mph on the road, it has considerable versatility; on optional "serious" off-road tires (and with the option of additional ground clearance and de-coupling anti-roll bars) it would go where very few of its "soft-road" rivals could even look at. It even gets close to the acknowledged master of off-road performance, the Range Rover. As so often before, the reality of the product could stop the critics dead in their tracks, but it would take a great deal to stop the Cayenne itself.

Below: Although it is Porsche's first entry into the Sports Utility Vehicle market, the Cayenne is still a Porsche through and through. It combines typically strong design with a powerful engine and technological highlights.

Above: Four doors and five seats were a first for Porsche, and the Cayenne looks very different from any of their other models—but it is far more Sport than Utility.

Left: The dash features a comprehensive array of equipment. Porsche were used to building "lifestyle" cars—but the Cayenne aspires to a lifestyle that Porsche hadn't embraced before.

Left: Inside, it is roomy, comfortable and much more luxurious than functional. Despite this, the Cayenne has convinced the critics that Porsche can build an SUV that works.

Left: The compact, all-new, all-alloy 4.5-liter four-cam, four-valve V8 engine with VarioCam timing. In Turbo form it has a huge 450bhp and 475lb.ft of torque, making the Cayenne the fastest off-roader in the world with a maximum of 165mph and 0–60mph in 5.6 seconds.

Above: The off-roader that thinks it's a 911. Its on-road
handling is better than any other luxury sporting 4x4, while its
off-road capabilities are close to those of the acknowledged
master of off-road performance, the Range Rover.

SPECIFICATIONS

Engine V10, water-cooled
Capacity 5700cc
Bore x stroke 98.0 x 76.0mm
Compression ratio 12.0:1
Power 603bhp
Valve gear Four overhead camshafts, four valves per cylinder, continuously variable inlet and exhaust valve timing
Fuel system Sequential multi-point fuel injection
Transmission Six-speed manual
Front suspension Double wishbones, horizontal coil spring and telescopic damper units, anti-roll bar
Rear suspension Double wishbones, horizontal coil spring and telescopic damper units, anti-roll bar
Brakes All PCCB Porsche Ceramic Composite Brake discs, cross drilled, ABS
Wheels Forged magnesium, center-lock
Weight 3041lb. (1380kg)
Maximum speed 205mph (328kph)
Production Production version unveiled March 2003

Carrera GT

Above: The Carrera GT was unveiled as a roadgoing concept car at the Paris Show in September 2000. Even with a putative price tag of almost a quarter of a million pounds sterling, potential buyers were soon queuing to commit their deposits.

Below: Even with its ferocious performance, the Carrera GT is designed to be practical and comfortable, with usable front luggage space and special seats with added knee and leg support.

After the 911 GT1 finally won the Le Mans race that it was primarily designed for (at its third attempt, in 1998), the natural assumption was that Porsche would continue to contest the 24-hour classic—even though changing rules and ever tougher competition would mean creating another new car to eclipse even that "ultimate 911." That was as Porsche intended, but largely thanks to the pressure of developing not only new models but (in the Cayenne for example) exploring new directions, it didn't happen. In classic Porsche style, though, work already done wasn't wasted; racing's loss would become the roadgoing range's gain—as the stillborn Le Mans car re-emerged as an all-new supercar, powered by a radical departure for Porsche, in a completely new engine configuration.

As the Carrera GT, it was unveiled as a roadgoing concept car at the Paris Show in September 2000—an open two-seater roadster with the mechanical layout of a racer and the up-market looks and equipment of a luxury grand tourer. This was Porsche climbing right back to the top of the supercar tree, head to head again with arch rivals from the likes of Ferrari, Lamborghini, the forthcoming McLaren-developed Mercedes SLR, the Bugatti Veyron, and newcomer Pagani. It promised to be the most extreme Porsche road car of all, eclipsing even the million-dollar race-clone 911 GT1, and like the GT1 it would have genuine race-bred credentials—even if it had never actually raced.

It bristled with leading edge technology, and the classic combination of maximum power in minimum weight. It was longer and wider than a 911, but with its carbonfiber and aluminum chassis and body structure it was lighter, with all-up weight, even in what promised to be fully-equipped road trim, of only around 2976lbs. (1350kg), road ready. For the Carrera GT, that would also mean leather trim, air-conditioning, a removable targa top, electric windows and a version of the concept car's multi-function electronic instrumentation, just for starters.

The Carrera GT was designed to be practical, too, and comfortable even given its ferocious performance—so, for instance, it included some usable luggage space at the front, and special seats with some additional knee and leg support.

All of which had been intriguing enough as a concept car but became even more so when, in echoes of Gruppe B and Boxster concepts, reaction to the Paris show car ensured Porsche would turn the Carrera GT concept into roadgoing reality. In fact, even given a putative price tag of almost a quarter of a million pounds sterling, potential buyers were soon queuing up to commit their deposits. So at the Detroit Show in January 2002 Porsche confirmed that they really would build it, with a promised "production" launch towards the spring of 2003, after an official unveiling at the Geneva Show in March.

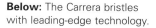

Below: The Carrera bristles with leading-edge technology.

Power wouldn't be an issue. As finalized for production, the mid-mounted engine was a super-lightweight, super-compact 5.7-liter V10—Porsche's first example of what had become a classic racing layout. This high-revving, four-cam 40-valve unit (developed by the racing department and featuring such exotic touches as titanium conrods and VarioCam valve timing) promised 603bhp, with close to 450lb.ft. torque. It would drive through a "ceramic composite" clutch and six-speed manual transmission, with a high-mounted double-H-gate gearshift very close to the steering wheel—but resisting the option of paddle shifts or one-touch sequential operation. And the Carrera GT would be rear-drive only, for a traditional handling balance and maximum purity of feel and response, with the safety net of a high-threshold variant of the electronic PSM Porsche Stability Management. That would be reassuring in a car promising a maximum of 205mph, and 0–60mph in comfortably under four seconds.

The rest was equally focused, including race-style all wishbone "pushrod" suspension, with driver-adjustable settings and the rear units mounted directly to the engine and transmission. Porsche's traditional braking performance would be provided by eight-pot brake calipers and ceramic composite discs—again directly descended from racing developments. And with such performance, aerodynamic aids would include a lifting rear wing and underbody "diffuser," for positive downforce and maximum stability at high speed.

Unlike the GT1, which only ever ran to a handful of customer cars and an even smaller handful of roadgoing examples, the Carrera GT would be a genuine series-built model—albeit in a series restricted to 1000 cars, all left-hand drive, and to be hand built (in the same new production facility as the Cayenne, in Leipzig) over a planned production program of around three years. For Porsche, there are times when even *not* racing can improve the breed.

Left: The mid-mounted engine—a super-lightweight, super-compact 5.7-liter V10. This high-revving, four-cam 40-valve unit was developed by the racing department and features such exotic touches as titanium conrods and VarioCam valve timing. It promised 603bhp, with close to 450lb.ft. torque.

Above: The concept car has multi-functional electronic instrumentation.

Above: The interior has the up-market good looks and equipment of a luxury grand tourer.

Left: Its carbonfiber and aluminum chassis makes the Carrera GT light, even with leather trim, air-conditioning, removable targa top, and electric windows.

A sporting life—Porsche in motor sport

If you consider not just one or two specialized branches of motor sport, but the whole scene, from rallying to Grand Prix racing, from Le Mans to America's ovals, few companies, if any, can match the breadth and depth of Porsche's half-century-plus of achievements. Maybe that shouldn't come as a big surprise. After all, Professor Porsche was involved in racing design all his working life, from his early days with Austro Daimler to his prewar GP designs for Auto Union. Even the birth of the Porsche marque itself, in 1948, was largely funded by Porsche's work on the Cisitalia GP car. So it shouldn't have been any surprise that once Porsche began to build cars, it would soon start to race them. In fact, within weeks of the first Porsche being completed it had taken a class win in a minor race in Austria, thanks largely to the characteristics that had made that original 356 such an unfeasibly rapid road car—that is, light weight, a slippery shape, and clever engineering. And having started its competition campaigns with a production-based sports car, Porsche made such cars the enduring core of its achievements ever since—with one race above all putting the marque's greatness beyond doubt.

Since the Le Mans 24-Hour race began in 1923, no manufacturer has won the endurance classic more times than Porsche. Probably none ever will. Even beyond their sixteen outright victories between 1970 and 1998, Porsche has a record of other statistics that stands head and shoulders above their nearest rivals. Up to 2002, according to Le Mans records, 677 Porsches had started the race and 321 had been classified as finishers. That's a better than 47 per cent finishing record. It's also 408 more starts than next-up Ferrari, and 226 more finishes. But that's only the bones of the story, because Porsche and Le Mans are inseparable.

It started in 1951, with a single 356 coupe driven by two young Frenchmen—Porsche importer August Veuillet and his friend Edmond Mouchet. There should have been another 356 but it crashed in testing and didn't start. Veuillet and Mouchet, however, did finish, in twentieth place, having spent the shortest time in the pits of any car in that year's race. More importantly, they won the 1100cc class, and through the rest of the 1950s, as Jaguar, Mercedes and Ferrari took the lion's share of outright wins, Porsche had at least one class win every year except 1959, when there was an upset at the head of the race

Opposite Top: Porsche's forays into single-seater racing in the early 1960s were far less successful than their efforts with sports cars, but even the 1962 Type 804 F1 car is undeniably stylish.

Opposite Bottom: The Cisitalia GP car that Porsche designed for Argentine industrialist Piero Dusio. It was technically advanced but never raced in anger. It did, however, play a major role in funding the Porsche company.

Left: The start of something very big. Porsche's first appearance at Le Mans, in 1951, with the Veuillet and Mouchet 356 coupe.

Below: It wasn't all circuit racing, even in the early days. A 356 Speedster made a reasonably civilized rally car in the days when rallying was a rather gentler sport—and Buchet and Storez naturally won the 1957 Mont-Blanc Iseran Rally.

too, with Carroll Shelby and Roy Salvadori's Aston Martin beating hot favorites Ferrari.

By then, with successive versions of the 356 and the competition-bred 550, RS and RSK, Porsches had won the 1100 and 1500 classes, the Index of Performance, and in 1958 the 2-liter class they would soon make their own. That first 2-liter win was by Jean Behra and Hans Hermann in an RSK. They also finished third overall for Porsche's first visit to the Le Mans podium, with Edgar Barth and Paul Frère fourth in another RSK winning the 1500 class, and Godin de Beaufort and Herbert Linge fifth in an RS, on a fine weekend in which five Porsches started and four finished.

1959 apart, when six Porsches out of six failed, for the next thirty years there would be Porsches in the frame whenever the checkered flag fell on Sunday afternoon at Le Mans, either as class winners or, soon, as outright winners—and the path to that had already begun.

By 1960 Porsche had almost a decade's experience building pure competition cars, which were getting bigger in capacity, faster and even more competitive. The 1960s was a decade of classic models, starting with the four-cylinder RS60s and GS Abarths, joined in 1963 by the glorious 2-liter flat-eight 718s, from 1964 by the 904 in four-, six- and eight-cylinder versions, and from 1966 by the six-cylinder, fuel-injected, spaceframed 906—still initially in the 2-liter class but taking full advantage of the latest "prototype" rules to edge ever closer to the ultimate prize.

With drivers of the caliber of Masten Gregory, Herbert Linge, Barth and Hermann, Guy Ligier, Jo Siffert, Rolf Stommelen, Jochen Neerspach, Vic Elford and Gerard Larrousse, and the 907, 908 and 910 racers, Porsche continued to pile up the class wins through the 1960s. But although they also pushed hard at the front, the decade only saw two actual winning marques, as Ford took on Ferrari in a battle of money and technology even Porsche couldn't hope to beat—for the moment.

One Porsche tradition had already begun at Le Mans. In 1966 Jean Kerguen and "Franc" gave the 911 its first 24-Hour outing and finished 14th overall—which wasn't bad, although it could hardly have led anyone to imagine that derivatives of the 911 would still be competitive at Le Mans, and still winning classes, more than 35 years on. Then, as the 1970s dawned, Porsche's day as outright Le Mans winners finally dawned too.

By now, the technology at Le Mans was second only to GP racing, and when the rules changed again, Porsche were ready for them. As Ford and Ferrari stepped back, Porsche prepared to pounce. In 1969 they unveiled one of the greatest racing cars of all time, the 917.

Above: Early days in another speciality—the winning 356 of Boutin and Motte setting a new record on the Rousset hillclimb section of the Lyons Charbonnier Rally.

Amazingly, it wasn't classified as a prototype. The 3-liter 908s were prototypes, and quick enough to take the world sports car title from Ferrari. The 917, though, was designed principally to win Le Mans, and by lining up 25 identical examples for official inspection at the Stuttgart factory, Porsche qualified it as a production car—albeit one with a 4.5-liter air-cooled flat-12 and around 585bhp in a spaceframe chassis designed purely for racing. In its early form it was savagely powerful and evil handling but already immensely quick. The main reason it didn't win Le Mans first time out, in 1969, was that it was barely ready to race at all. Its wild reputation was underlined, too, before the end of the first lap, when John Woolfe's privately entered 917 got away from its experienced driver, crashed in flames and killed Woolfe instantly. For 20 hours, though, the works cars dominated the race—then failed, leaving the Gulf Ford GT40 to pip Hermann and Larrouse's 908 by just yards.

In 1970 nothing could touch the 917. The 24 Porsches entered included seven short- and long-tail 4.5 and 4.9-liter 917s, in various team colors. Ferry Porsche dropped the starter's flag, and 24 hours later Porsche, starting from pole, had a 1-2-3 win, led by Hans Hermann and Dickie Attwood. Porsche also set a new outright lap record and won every capacity class plus the Sports, GT and Prototype classes, Indexes of Performance, and Thermal Efficiency, and World Championship of Makes. Then in 1971 Helmut Marko and Gijs van Lennep won with the 917K, before the 5-liter monsters were outlawed by a switch to a 3-liter formula which for the next few years favored F1-cloned Le Mans cars like the Matra, and the Cosworth-powered Gulf Mirage. So for a while, the Porsche flag was flown mainly by ever-wilder 911 derivatives, now with turbocharging and colossal power in extreme aerodynamic bodywork.

In various guises the 911s (and 934s and 935s) ran in Group 4, Group 5, GT, GTX and IMSA—and won more or

less as they pleased, in a decade where every Le Mans grid appeared to be dominated by Porsches of one sort or another. In 1976 when Ickx and van Lennep took Porsche back to the winner's circle with the 936, 26 Porsches started and fourteen finished. When Ickx, Barth and Haywood gave the 936 another win in 1977, 25 started. In 1979 there were twenty on the grid, the 935s (especially Kremer's K3s) were the cars to beat, and Klaus Ludwig and the American Whittington brothers won from Dick Barbour, Rolf Stommelen, and Paul Newman—the latter outdoing Steve McQueen, who in 1969 had only acted the part for his famous Le Mans film (driving a 917, of course).

Through the 1980s, starting with Ickx and Derek Bell's 1981 win in the 936/81, Porsche won seven Le Mans in a row—with the 936, 956, 962, and drivers including Ickx and Bell again, Al Holbert, Hurley Haywood, Vern Schuppan, Klaus Ludwig, Henri Pescarolo, Paolo Barilla, "John Winter" and Hans Stuck. It was the longest winning streak in the history of the race, but until 1994 it was Porsche's swansong. Pushed out in the meantime by Jaguar, Mercedes, Mazda and Peugeot, they bounced back in 1994—with the apparently outdated Porsche-powered Dauer 962LM GT1 beating all the prototypes, in the hands of Dalmas, Haywood and Mauro Baldi.

There were three more Porsche wins in the 1990s. Manuel Reuter, Davy Jones and Alexander Wurz, then Michele Alboreto, Stefan Johansson and Tom Kristensen took back to back wins for the Joest TWR Porsche WSC in 1996 and 1997, when all logic said the ultimate development of the 911, the 911 GT1, should have won easily. In 1998 it finally did win, at its third attempt, driven by Allan McNish, Laurent Aiello and Stephane Ortelli. It was Porsche's sixteenth outright Le Mans win in the marque's fiftieth year. And to date, their last, as the works GT1s never returned to Le Mans.

2001 was another milestone, fifty years on from the marque's first appearance at the race. Sadly, for the second year running there were no works cars to chase outright victory against Audi and Bentley, but the 911 GT3s still outnumbered any other single model in any class, and naturally they won the GT category—with the GT3-RS of Gabrio Rosa, Luca Drudi and Fabio Babini sneaking home in sixth place overall as atrocious conditions sidelined more obvious front runners. It was much the same, too, in 2002, when the 911 GT3-RSs were still the class of the GT field and dominated the category yet again, taking the top five places in the GT class.

And although it's a while since Porsche has been involved in the battle for outright honors, it would be a brave man who'd bet against the marque ever coming back in search of outright victory, and perhaps taking it. Because that's too strong a heritage to abandon forever...

Although Le Mans is the race that grabs all the headlines, though, Porsche's broader achievements in sports car racing stretch way beyond that, not least with multiple wins in two more endurance classics on the far side of the Atlantic—a record seventeen outright victories in the 12 Hours of Sebring and eighteen in the Daytona 24 Hours. And they go beyond only traditional endurance racing—or even circuit racing—because Porsche has also had a hugely successful career in the epic road races, in shorter circuit races, in hillclimbs, even in rallying.

As at Le Mans, too, the marque's record in the great road racing classics like the Mille Miglia, Targa Florio and Carrera Panamericana is unrivalled. The first class win in the Mille Miglia came in 1952, for Count Johnny Lurani's 356 in the 1500 class, and the main reason Porsche didn't achieve multiple outright wins in that race was that the event itself was outlawed as too dangerous before the opportunity arose. The same could be said about the

Top: In the golden years of the 1970s and 1980s, Porsche frequently dominated the Le Mans 24-Hour race. This is Ickx and van Lennep's turbocharged 936 en route to victory in 1976—the third of Ickx's record six Le Mans wins, and van Lennep's second.

Above: All conquering 908/02, airborne over one of the many yumps of the Nurburgring, in the days when there were more trees than crash barriers and the spectators were very close to the action.

Left: The other side of the fence—preparations in the Porsche garage for the 1978 Le Mans race. For once they were beaten, by Renault.

exceptionally tough Carrera Panamericana, which is, of course, commemorated in one of Porsche's most famous model names. There, Porsche opened its account in 1953 with a 1500 class win for José Herrarte. And in the final running of the Carrera, in 1954, a remarkable third place overall against far bigger and supposedly faster cars (and another class win) for Hans Hermann's 550 Spyder showed what might have been if that race, too, had been allowed to continue.

In the one great road race that did survive for rather longer, the Targa Florio, Porsche's unbeaten record of eleven outright wins and countless class wins is astonishing given the strength of the opposition. That began in 1956, when Umberto Maglioli won outright with a legendary single-handed effort in the 550. Barth and Seidel won in 1959, Bonnier and Hermann in 1960, and Bonnier and

Opposite Top: The legendary 917 in the evocative colors of Gulf Racing in 1970, driven here by one of the few men who could genuinely tame it—Pedro Rodriguez, who could even make the 917 work in the wet.

Opposite Inset: Lovingly preserved—the same car in the same instantly recognizable colors more than thirty years later.

Opposite Bottom: In the 1970s and 1980s, Porsche usually had more than one string to their bow in top class sports car racing. This is one of Kremer's Group 5 935s leading a 936 from the prototype class at Brands Hatch in 1980.

Carlo Abate in 1963—with other Porsche drivers adding further wins right through to 1973, when Muller and van Lennep won the final running of the Targa, in a 911 RSR.

Over six decades, all this has brought championships as well as individual race wins, including every major title in world sports car racing, from World Endurance Championship to World Sportscar Championship, the European GT Championship to the World Championship for Sportscar Manufacturers, the Group C World Championship, and countless victories in the prestigious American IMSA GT Championship.

In the even more specialized arena of the European Hillclimb Championship, too, Porsche came to dominate, with some twenty titles in various classes—again thanks to cars which took the philosophy of light weight and brilliant chassis dynamics to its extremes.

As for rallying, Porsche made its official debut in the same year it debuted at Le Mans, 1951—when Paul von Guilleaume's 356 finished third overall and won the 1500 class in the grueling Liège-Rome-Liège rally. A year later, Helmut Polensky and Walter Schluter's 356 coupe won the same rally outright while the team also added the Alpine and Sestrière rallies, and in 1954 Maleric and Cerne won the Acropolis as Polensky and Schluter completed a great year by taking the European Rally title.

In 1965, the 911, like the 356, made a class-winning rally debut, in the most famous of all rallies, the Monte Carlo, where Herbert Linge and Peter Falk took fifth overall and the 2-liter class-win. Two years later Vic Elford and David Stone won the GT class in the Monte in another 911 before winning outright in 1968. That win was repeated by Bjorn Waldegard and Lars Helmer in

Below: Another classic Porsche in classic colors—the 962C of the Rothmans-backed factory team, driven at the Silverstone 1000km race in 1985 by Derek Bell and Hans Joachim Stuck. A couple of weeks later they took the same car to third place at Le Mans, behind two 956s.

Left: It wasn't only the works team that kept the 962 in the forefront of world class sports car racing. By the late 1980s the 962 "customer" teams were also forces to be reckoned with. This is Bob Wollek and Phillip Streiff in Joest Racing's version in 1988.

Below Opposite: What was intended to be. The circuit racing version of the 959 was dubbed the 961, but its career was short-lived, and ended by rules that didn't help it at all. Rene Metge and Claude Ballot-Lena did finish seventh at Le Mans in 1986, though, behind five 962s and 956s, and a lone 936.

1969, when they also won the Swedish rally to retain the European Rally title for Porsche. Pauli Toivonen had won that the year before, as the 911 began to be the car to beat in the snow, on gravel and in the forest as well as on the racetrack. In 1970, Waldegaard and Helmer confirmed its ability by completing the 911's Monte Carlo hat-trick, and a second successive Swedish win. Then a decade after its first Monte win, and long after most of the cars it had been competing against then had been retired, in 1978, reveling in snowy conditions that caught out many others, a privately-entered 911 crewed by Jean-Pierre Nicolas and Vincent Laverne scored an amazing fourth outright Monte win for the 911 in an age where the specialist rally car was supposedly already king.

The works, too, came back to rallying in the 1980s— or at least to the even more extreme discipline of "rally-raids," when they took on the challenge of the Paris-Dakar with "Gruppe B" prototypes of the 959, before the Group B category was axed and the 959's real competition career was brought to an end before it had started. What it did achieve, though, showed what might

have been. In 1984 Porsche entered three of the turbocharged four-wheel-drive supercars and Rene Metge with Antoine Lemoine won the event outright—the "959" also winning the Rally of the Pharaohs across Egypt. Admittedly they were less successful in 1985 when none of the three cars entered in the Paris-Dakar finished, but in 1986, just before Group B was outlawed forever, they scored a spectacular Paris-Dakar one-two, with Metge winning again, just ahead of Jacky Ickx—the multiple Le Mans winner and GP driver who had suggested the Paris-Dakar program to Porsche in the first place.

Then there was the Canadian-American Challenge Cup—Can-Am, which was like sports car racing on steroids. And nobody pumped its Can-Am cars up more than Porsche did in the 1970s. They went to the American series first as an alternative to the European-based FIA World Sportscar Championship, when rule changes in that series didn't suit the directions Porsche was developing in. And as they had everywhere else, they soon started winning. In 1971 they created an open, spyder version of the 917 with a turbocharged flat-12 giving prodigious

power even by previous 917 standards. Having first put a foot in the Can-Am water during 1969 and 1970, they got serious about the series in 1971 with the first of the turbocharged 917/10s, and in 1972 won their first Can-Am title, with George Follmer driving (after team mates Jo Siffert had been killed in a F1 accident and Mark Donohue had been injured in America). Donohue had recovered by 1973, though, and added another Can-Am title for the 917/30—which now developed more than 1100bhp and would top 250mph. And although Porsche's Can-Am campaign ended as the rules changed slightly, essentially the same cars added two more titles in 1974 and 1975—in the European version of Can-Am, the Interserie championship, led by prolific winners Leo Kinnunen, Georg Loos and Willy Kauhsen.

But Porsche have also been successful almost without being noticed. Oddly perhaps, the least visibly successful racing discipline for Porsche has been single-seaters—but all things are relative and even in the open-wheel formulae there are actually few areas where Porsche hasn't won, or helped its partners to win. And that includes Formula 1.

Porsche finally arrived in F1 in 1961, via sports car racing and F2—the final catalyst being the introduction of the 1.5-liter F1 GP formula, which suited the usual size of Porsche engine rather better than the previous 2.5-liter formula. The first of the F2 cars had appeared in 1957 when the junior category was revived, also for 1.5-liter cars—and the first F2 Porsches were single-seaters, but not open-wheelers, because there was nothing in the rules that said they had to be, and Porsche as ever would make maximum use of slippery aerodynamics.

So the first three (which were in effect Spyder RSs with one seat covered over, and powered by 145bhp versions of the four-cam flat-four) were hastily prepared for the F2 class of the German Grand Prix, at the Nurburgring in August. They would run alongside the

rather thin F1 entry but without being eligible for World Championship points, and face six genuine F2 Cooper-Climax single seaters, which were lighter if no more powerful, and certainly less aerodynamic. And after an epic battle with the Coopers, the race provided Porsche's first ever single-seater win, as Edgar Barth benefited from Salvadori's Cooper breaking its suspension.

It didn't exactly start a flood of success, the F2 cars didn't even appear again in 1957, but in July 1958 Jean Behra won the F2 event at the Grand Prix of Europe at Reims—in an RSK Spyder based car converted from the car that had finished fourth overall at Le Mans two weeks earlier.

The sports based F2 cars were also quick enough to give Barth second place at the Nurburgring in 1958, alongside the F1 cars, and for Masten Gregory to win the F2 finale at the super-fast Avus track.

Then, with a new 1500cc F1 formula due for 1961, Porsche started to make its first proper single-seater open-wheel racing cars, which won at Reims in 1959 and at Aintree, Nurburgring, Zeltweg, Capetown and Modena in 1960 to take the Constructors' Championship and the unofficial F2 drivers' championship as the car developed towards a new F1 role.

In its debut year, the 1961 flat-four Porsche GP car, driven by Dan Gurney, Jo Bonnier, Hans Hermann and de Beaufort took third place in the F1 constructors' championship, behind Ferrari and Lotus. Unfortunately, as the Porsche F1 cars developed over the next couple of years, the opposition developed even faster, and it wasn't until the flat-eight-engined 804 appeared in 1962 that Porsche had a real, modern GP car. It was too late, though—the rest had moved on too far, and although the car scored a historic championship Grand Prix win for Porsche at Rouen in July, driven by Gurney, it would prove to be Porsche's one and only GP win as a constructor. Gurney won another non-championship GP a couple of

weeks later, at Solitude, but for once the costs of racing didn't justify the results, and the US GP at Watkins Glen was Porsche's last F1 outing.

It was a long time before they tried single seaters again, and when they did it was in the American CART series in 1979, but the comeback was short-lived, as late rule changes for 1980 made Porsche's turbocharged Indy car uncompetitive and the project was quietly abandoned.

The next single-seater involvement was rather more successful. In 1983 Porsche returned to GP racing for the first time since the 1960s, not this time as a full-scale car manufacturer but as an engine supplier to one of the most respected teams in the sport. The team was McLaren, the engine Porsche designed, developed and built on behalf of Techniques Avant Garde was the 1.5-liter V6 TAG Turbo. And in the back of successive generations of McLaren, it won three successive drivers' and two constructors' championships, in dominant style. In 1984 it took Niki Lauda to the title and scored a record number of wins for a single season—twelve of the sixteen rounds. In 1985 and 1986 it powered Alain Prost to back-to-back championships, but by 1986 Williams were close enough to beat it to the constructors' title. Prost won three more races in 1987, but then, as they often do when they are slipping from the very top of the game, Porsche walked away again, to find a different challenge.

In 1988 that should have seen a return to the American alternative to GP racing, with another foray into Indycars. And this time Porsche was planning to go the whole way, with a complete car and engine package rather than just as an engine supplier, and a V8 quite closely related to the F1 TAG V6 Turbo. The plan, though, was cut short again before it had time to come to fruition— tragically, this time after team boss and former Le Mans winner Al Holbert was killed in a light airplane crash.

It wasn't quite the end of the program, though, as Porsche (having realized that this time their own chassis was the weakest link) compromised and fitted the V8 turbo into a single-seater chassis jointly developed with ultra-successful British constructors March. And it still wasn't a huge success, but the powerful engine did prove to be a winner, as Teo Fabi won one Indycar race in 1989 at Mid-Ohio, with what had by then become the Quaker State Porsche. Then they walked away again.

Maybe most important of all, in motor sport worldwide, Porsche has been involved in almost every category at every level since the company was founded, scoring literally thousands wins in total and forming the bedrock of many categories and race series. In fact with a competition career now fast approaching its fortieth year, the 911 alone, in all its guises, is such an icon that there are enthusiasts who have never seen a major sports car race without a 911, and certainly drivers who have never known racing without a 911 snapping at their heels. Motor sport has been very good for Porsche, but Porsche has been great for motor sport.

Opposite: The greatest success for anything closely related to the 959 was in long-distance "rally-raids" and notably the Paris-Dakar, where the Group B version of the car was a winner. This is a 959 during testing.

Below: For now, Porsche's final fling in the top level of sports car racing has been the 911GT1. It won Le Mans in 1998 at its third attempt—and then the works walked away from racing. But probably not forever...

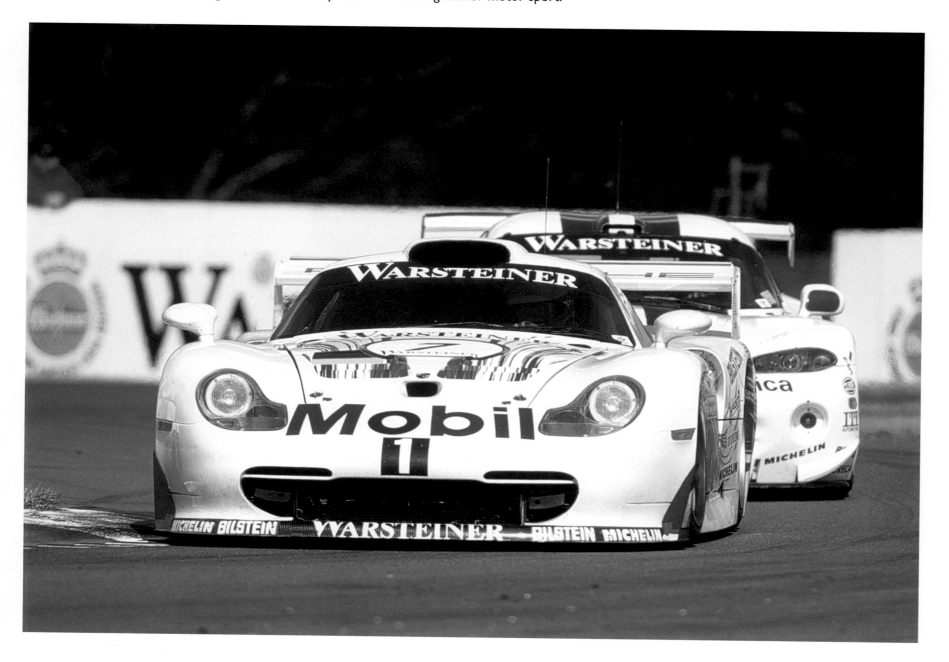

Credits